TI⸺⸺⸺⸺ ᴏꜰ THE WORLD

VOL. I

THE HOLY INFANCY

By

Charlotte M. Mason

This book is Part One in a multi-volume set
of poetry covering the life of Christ.

Reprinted June 2015

Minor alterations have been made to the content by the
current Publisher. The painting reproductions in the original
were left out. The original text did not have subheadings—
the descriptions used in the Index were added to each section
to serve as titles/sub-headings for clarity while reading.

ISBN-13: 978-1514359792
ISBN-10: 1514359790

THE SAVIOUR OF THE WORLD

VOL. I

THE HOLY INFANCY

CONTENTS

APOLOGIA

A traveller passed the sign of the "Rising Sun":
  Smiling at yellow paint in flaming rays,
He thought of the Sun: seeing, his journey done,
  A "Dawn" by Claude, the Picture had his praise.

INTRODUCTORY

We are at present in a phase of religious thought, Christian or pseudo-Christian, when a synthetic study of the life and teaching of Christ may well be of use. We have analysed until the mind turns in weariness from the broken fragments; we have criticised until there remains no new standpoint for the critic; but if we could only get a *whole* conception of Christ's life among men, and of the philosophic method of His teaching, His own word should be fulfilled, and the Son of Man, lifted up, would draw all men unto himself.

It seems to the writer that *verse* offers a comparatively new medium in which to present the great theme. It is more impersonal, more condensed, and is capable of more reverent handling than is prose; and what Wordsworth calls "The authentic comment" may be essayed in verse with more becoming diffidence. Again, the supreme moment of a very large number of lives—that in which a person is brought face to face with Christ—comes before us with great vividness in the gospel narratives; and it is possible to treat what we call dramatic situations with more force, and, at the same time, more reticence, in verse than in prose.

Indeed, the gospel story offers the epic of the ages for the poet who shall arise in the future, strong in faith, and meek enough to hold his creative gift in reverent subjection. We have a single fragment of this great epic:—

"those holy fields,
Over whose acres walk'd those blessed feet
which, fourteen hundred years ago, were nailed,
For our advantage, on the bitter cross";—

If Shakespeare had given us the whole, how rich should we be! Every line of verse dealing directly with our

Lord from the standpoint of His Personality is greatly treasured. We love the lines in which Trench tells us,—

"Of Jesus sitting by Samarian well,
Or teaching some poor fishers on the shore";

and Keble's,—

"Meanwhile He paces through the adoring crowd,
Calm as the march of some majestic cloud";

or his,—

"In His meek power He climbs the mountain's brow."

Every line of such verse is precious, but the lines are few; no doubt because the subject is supremely august; but also, perhaps, because those poets who have written at length of *The Messiah*, have not left us words spoken out of the insight of faith upon which the soul can feed.

But the subject is as inspiring as it is august, and is of such surpassing interest that the *poet* need bring little more to his task than the equipment of passionate conviction: he will have power, too, to discern the unique psychological truth of every phrase of the narrative, as well as the amazing self-revelation of each speaker and actor. As regards the Divine Person, he will perceive that he cannot see for the brightness, cannot know for the greatness, but must needs adore and delight in the unspeakable loveliness as an insect basks in the sun.

He, the poet of the future who shall give the world its great epic, will perceive with the mediæval Church that the "Seven Liberal Arts" themselves are under the immediate inspiration of the Holy Ghost; that our knowledge of science comes to us in set portions at set times, according as we are ready and there is a man to be found with the hearing ear and the seeing eye. He will see that it is absurd to bring our fragmentary, inconclusive science into opposition with Him who sustains us with knowledge as with bread, and to say that this or that cannot be, before we are able to discern why and how anything that is exists. He will know that all these chimeras vanish as shapes of darkness before the Light of the World. It is a *poet* the world is waiting for; another greater Shakespeare, able to tell us the truth about Jesus Christ—That truth set so plainly before us in the Book we are forgetting how to read!

We know how the Tate and Brady version of the Psalms wrought a great religious revival, not only in England, but throughout Western Europe; we know, too, how Marot's Psalms fired the hearts of the Netherlanders to their heroic resistance. If new presentations of the Psalms have effected great things, what may not the Church expect when a poet shall be inspired to writ the epic of Christ?

It may be said, we have the whole story in the Gospels, and cannot hope or desire to improve upon that which is written. But this is true, also, of the Psalms; no poet's version can equal the original; a version in a new form is a concession to human infirmity, but we know how arresting a new, though inferior, presentation is; no one can read the Gospels in another tongue, though in a poorer translation, without new convictions, new delight. For these reasons, the writer ventures to hope that a rendering in verse which aims at no more than being faithful and reverent may give pleasure to Christian people, may help to bring out the philosophical sequence of our Lord's teaching, and throw into relief the incidents of His life.

The writer, at any rate, experiences in the study a curious and delightful sense of harmonious development, of the rounding out of each incident, of the progressive unfolding which characterises our Lord's teaching; and perhaps some measure of this entrancing interest may have found its way into this little volume. When the great poet shall give us the Great Christian Epic, it will be read in the closet and in the congregation, by the neophyte and the saint: in the meantime, a feeble attempt (made with anxious diffidence) *may* be of a little use in furthering that era of passionate Christianity which will probably be the world's next great experience, when "the shout of a King" shall be in our midst. If such attempt send any one back to a more diligent and delighted perusal of the sacred text, its end will be fully accomplished.

The scope of this work, *The Saviour of the World*, is to cover each incident and each saying in a single poem, blank verse or rhymed stanza, according to the subject. The poems follow one another in a time sequence, but each is distinct and separable. Therefore, though the work will, God willing, continue through a series of little Christmas volumes, each volume will be complete in itself and independent of the rest.

The first of these called *The Holy Infancy*, from the first of the three Books it contains, covers about an eighth of the whole subject; so it is probable that the work will be completed in eight such volumes.

The writer begs to acknowledge her great indebtedness to the Rev. C. C. James's *Gospel History*, combining the four Gospels (in the words of the Revised Version), which she has followed for the chronological order of events.

CHARLOTTE MASON
AMBLESIDE 1907

BOOK I

THE HOLY INFANCY

I

PROLOGUE TO THE GOSPEL
ACCORDING TO ST. JOHN

Intimate, searching, inly witnessing
In every heart of Man, behold, the Word!

We know not whence we came; nor how became:
The Word was in the beginning, and was God.

We may not know; but may know Him who knows;
For with the Word have all men secret speech.

The Word with the Father was ere time began:
He tells us of the Father all we know.

When came the world, and how were all things made?
All things that be to-day are of the Word.

No longer baffled, we, by tortuous quest—
Whether all life proceed from two or many,
Whether our origins be high or low—
Those things concern the manner of our making:
In Him was life; that is enough to know:
How He dispersed the largess of His bounty,
'T were good indeed to learn; and time will come
When ear to hear the whisper of the Word
Shall wake; a man, learned in the laws of things,
That he heard whispered by the Word, shall tell.
Till then we wait, not knowing whence we came,
But knowing Him from whom all doth proceed.

Nothing of all good things that have been made,
Picture, or world, or book, without Him came.

Nor knowledge good for man can mankind know,
But he vouchsafes it: He is all our light.

And every man who comes into the world
By that true light is lighted, knowing it not.

The light in darkness shone; darkness nor quench'd
Nor caught the light, but dark in the light remained.

He came unto the world that He had made,
And the world knew not Him, its life and light.

He came to His own people, called of Him,
And they that were His own received Him not.

As many as received Him, they became
Children of God, believing on His Name.

Our flesh the Word became, and dwelt with us,
And we beheld His glory, as, of God,
The only-begotten Son: we who believed
Knew glory when we saw it, by the signs—
Not of the pomp and majesty of Kings—
But Grace, the touch of God, showed sweet in Him;
And Truth, discerning all things, made Him simple,
His glory saw we—full of grace and truth.

II

THE EXPECTATION OF THE NATIONS

Conflict, disaster, ceased: the Earth was still
As one who holds his breath: proud souls and meek
Waited the Expectation of the Nations.

A rustle under foot when none doth move,
Peals overhead when skies are blue and high,
Warm breath on cheek when no man is in sight,—

As though by signs like these, were men perturbed:
All hearts uprose, as seas to meet the moon,
Questioning, uneasy, How t'abide the Coming?

No man could tell what he was looking for;
Each knew within himself a nameless need;
And souls, an-hungered, for appeasement cried.

THE ANGEL VISITS

An aged priest, within the temple courts,
In meditation watched the curling fumes—
His lot was to burn incense—and all the prayers
Of men he saw ascending; no, not all—
That prayer he prayed, and prayed again, for years,
He and his wife Elizabeth, had that
Indeed gone up to God?—A sudden gleam,
In that dim place, of light ineffable
Arrested him, and lo, an angel stood
At the right side of the altar:

                  "Fear not thou,"
The angelic word, for Zacharias trembled:
How had he dared to doubt? But not to chide
The visitor was sent: "Thy prayer is heard,"
(That very prayer of years ago he deemed
Had lost its way); 'thy wife Elizabeth
Shall carry babe in gladness; nor to her
And thee alone this joy (not any pair
May hold their child for all their own: but this)—
Many shall rejoice at his birth, for he
A great one in the sight of God shall be,
Filled with the Spirit from his mother's womb.
Give him not juice of grape, nor any drink
To cloud his clear intelligence of good:
His people shall he turn to God with the cry,
'Make ready, there, the highway for the King!'—
Whereat shall natural duties prick men's hearts;
Fathers bethink them of a son denied,
Children, of fathers recklessly defied—
Unseemly matters for the King to see—
And, rough made plain, behold the King's highway!
He goes before Messias to prepare,

As spake the prophets, a people for the Lord."

So said the seraph: Woe to the doubting heart!
No sudden generous impulse makes him sure—
Perchance, if he might see the wounds of Christ?
But lesser proof avails not, though it were
An angel fraught with promises should speak!
So, Zacharias: "How shall I know this thing?
I am an old man, and my wife is old;
Not for the aged are the joys of child-birth!"
To whom, austere, the seraph, grave rebuking:—
"I, Gabriel, who in the Presence stand,
Am sent by the Most High to thee with word
Of these glad tidings: be thou dumb, nor speak
Till all shall be fulfilled."
              So he went forth
Among the wondering people, making signs,
Whereby they knew an angel spake with him.
And, like an inlay in old cabinet,
His life a space of silence held, wherein
He spake with God, and was abash'd.

After these days Elizabeth conceived,
And for five months did hide herself from men
And praise God alway, Who, of His dear grace,
Shame and reproach had taken from her face.

COUNCIL IN HEAVEN

The great white throne was set; and therefrom spake
Jehovah, God almighty: heaven hush'd to hear:—

"Gabriel, who stand'st before the throne, art sent,
Wonted ambassador, to princely men
Who know to wrestle with their God, nor fall,

"Go thou on errand now to such a soul:
Meek maid thou'lt find, simple, of low estate,
Whose instant thought doth, as a fountain, rise:

"She wearieth heaven with importunity;
'Let a pure virgin of King David's house,'
So runs her prayer, 'be mother to the Babe!'

"Go thou to this one; say, 'Thus shall it be,—
Thyself shalt bear the Child, Son of the Highest,
Born in due time, the Saviour of the World.'"

SAGES AND PROPHETS PRAISE GOD FOR THE BIRTH

ISAIAH

Lo, that which I foretold!
"A Virgin shall conceive"—
But how might men believe
Thing never known of old?

"Immanuel, His name—
The very God with men":—
A word beyond my ken
Was given me to proclaim:

But, now, I see the whole—
The Babe, the Son, the Child,
The Lamb, all undefiled—
Now may I read the scroll

At one time I did write:
And, Wonderful His Name!
His majesty shall tame
Rebellious tribes; His might

Shall to all lands extend;
Under His government,
Men's hearts shall know content;
Of peace, shall be no end:

Holy, holy, holy,
Almighty Lord, my God!
Lo, this, the Branch, the Rod,—
Our God, an Infant lowly!

HAGGAI

"Desire of Nations" is His name!
And all the nations shall acclaim
Him King of kings and Lord of lords;
Peoples shall wait upon His words!

DANIEL

And I, who told the number'd days
Of waiting, learned not then Thy praise!
How wonderful Thy counsels, Lord,
How sure Thy all-fulfilling word!

MICAH

The secret of the place was mine
From out whose dimness Christ should
     shine:
But, Bethlehem, I—Esaias, Galilee—
How may these diverse words accomplish'd
     be?

PLATO

Of time and place, what need to know—
Is it that God indeed will show
The pattern of that perfect plan,
Distorted, blurr'd, in every man?

SOCRATES

But how shall man discern the Good?
Accepted not, nor understood,
The Christ Himself; should He show forth
The thoughts of heaven to sons of earth!

AESCHYLUS

Shall man, escaped, that fate elude,
Implacable, which him pursued?
Shall wistful souls Erinnes flee,
Not thwarted more by destiny?

VIRGIL

Is this the Boy,
Flower-cradled joy,
The Virgin Astraea should bring forth?
Smiling presage
Of the Golden Age
For all the labouring sons of earth!

SAGES AND PROPHETS

Shall every man have all the bliss
That is, by right of fitness, his?
Is Vision for all sons of men?
Shall peoples walk with God again?

But, oh, the head is sick, the heart
Too faint to choose the righteous part!
Shall the Messias purge the whole,
And animate each sinking soul?

And shall He in His power go forth?
From east and west, from south and north,
Shall men flock round Him with desire,
Soliciting His purging fire?

How wonderful Thy counsels, Lord
Thy ways past finding out, Thy word,

Quick and compelling, searcheth out
Just means to bring high ends about!

DAVID

Now may I, understanding, sing
That song indited to the King:
Fairer Thou art than sons of men,
Thy lips drop grace!—so ran my pen.

Gird Thee with sword, my mighty God,
Ride forth with spear, with bruising rod;
Because of meekness, truth, and right,
With piercing word, go forth to smite!

Thy Throne, O God, shall stand for aye;
Thy righteous sceptre, none defy;
Thou hatest wrong, Thou lovest right—
So God shall, late, in Man delight!

A Bridegroom, dight with majesty,
Kings' daughters haste to wait on Thee;
The Queen on Thy right hand doth stand,
Glorious in gold of Ophir's land.

All glorious, too, within is she,
Pure virgins her companions be;
With gifts and graces furnished
They go, the King's highway to spread!

.   .   .   .   .   .

Thus had I writ, nor understood
What manner of celestial good
My song foreshowed—revealed, the Word!
How wonderful Thy counsels, Lord!

VI

THE ANNUNCIATION

The angel Gabriel went forth once more
On that high errand: came to Nazareth,
Planted 'mid streams and trees, whose careless folk,
Content, in darkness sate—the shadow of death;
There dwelt a son of David Joseph named,
Betrothed to Mary, virgin of that house.

Alone upon the housetop knelt the maid;
Once more her urgent, passionate prayer she prayed—
"Send us Messias!"—when, lo, the angel came,
As friend, familiar, called her by her name.

"Hail, Mary!" said the seraph—in the word,
Angelic love and reverence were heard—
"All hail, thou happy virgin, full of grace,
Who hast high favour found before the face

"Of God; the Lord be with thee; fear not thou!"
For she was greatly troubled; questioned how
(Within herself) had she offended; hold—
Had she made her petitions over bold?

Gentle, he reassured her; "Nay, fear not!
No word of thine in heaven hath been forgot:
Thou shalt conceive, and bear a Holy Son,
The very Son of God; whose reign, begun

"Within thy womb, in time shall have no end,
And over all the tribes of men extend:
Jesus, His Name; the Son of God Most High,
Yet shall He on thy brest, and infant, lie!"

.   .   .   .   .   .

As men walk roth by day, nor ever know
That all the air with colour is aglow,
Till here, black clouds, and there, a blushing rose
Lend surface, hues of beauty to disclose;—

"The rose is red," then say they; "see the arc
The multi-coloured bow spreads o'er the dark
Rainclouds opposed to the sun!" Nor recognise
That all the purple, crimson, orange dyes

Are held in the white light, till broken rays
Let loose on this or that the hues they praise.
So is life held in God; nor needs, at best,
The will of any two to manifest.

"LET THERE BE LIFE," His primal word; and straight
His creatures lived; endowed to propagate
Each after his own kind: so men grew used
To the one way; and, all their thought obtused

By long-continued custom, ne'er foresaw
That He who made the first, a second Law
Might bring forth from His counsels—for a Birth,
Should quicken all the recreant sons of Earth!

Again the mandate issued: Be there life:—
And she whom no man yet had ta'en to wife
Conceived and bare a Son: the Virgin-born,
Come, after heavy night, the promised Morn!
But Mary understood not yet; nor we.

.   .   .   .   .   .

Not querulous, nor doubting—meekly, she,

Asking direction, did the angel show
That which perplexed her: "Seeing I no man know,
How shall this be after the wont of men?"
For great the mystery: the angel, then,
Showed how by immediate power of God Most High
The think should come to pass; and how thereby
The child born unto her should holy be,
THE SON OF GOD.
     Because her hallowed glee
Must in her heart lie hid, the angel, kind,
Perceiving that to tell would soothe her mind,
Spake of Elizabeth, and her great hap—
How she, grown old, should soon have child on lap—
For every word of God shall be with power.
And Mary—scarce perceiving all her hour
Might bring—"Behold the handmaid of the Lord!
Be it to me according to thy word."

VII

LUKE 1.33

CHILD of Art, Spirit-born,
 Our thanks we give
For the still holiness,
The fair child innocence,
For the worship embodied
 In thee that live!

Well was't to make thee rise,
 Thou woman pure!
Held by slight chain of sin,
Few earth-tied hopes within,
Drawn to Centre above thee,
 Thy course were sure!

Knowest how high thou art,
 God-seeking soul,
Above all earth's clamour,
Above the moon's glamour,
Above the thick clouds which still
 Over us roll?

Nay, thy Simplicity
 Knows not its state!
 Into thy joy's pure deep
Thought of self might not creep,
And leave thee unconscious still,
 Childlike and great.

In air we breathe not yet
 Thy soul doth soar;
We climb the heights of prayer
Only by efforts rare:—

But, higher thy dwelling-place,
     Thou dost adore!

The Power of the Highest
     'Tis thine to know:
In fearing the Mystery,
Adoring the Majesty,
And loving that Love supreme
     All thy powers flow.

What meed to the seer
     Who for men brought,
From the innermost shrine,
     'Neath the Shadow divine,
That face, in its purity
     Hushing our thought?

VIII

MEETING WITH ELIZABETH

MUCH troubled was the Maid—full of high hope
And diffident fear: nor might she tell her mind
To kin or neighbour, least of all, to him,
Her betrothed husband: so, with bold resolve,
She would go forth to seek among the hills
Of southward Judah for Elizabeth:
The friendly seraph, sure, had meant that she
Might ease her bosom in her kinswoman's arms!

Little she recked of distance, lonely ways,
Of days of travel, footsore and distressed,
And nights of little ease: Mary made slow way
To the hill-city, Hebron, where she dwelt
To reach whom all this travail. Entering the house
Of Zacharias, with sisterly salute,
Elizabeth she greeted.

             At her word,
Tumult of welcome whelme'd the poor Maid,
Lonely and travel-worn: when Elizabeth heard
Her cousin's salutation, in her womb
Up-leaped the babe: and, full of the Holy Ghost,

With a loud cry she lifted up her voice:—
"Thou blessed amongst women, whence is this,
That the Mother of my Lord should come to me?
No sooner had the babe I bear thy voice
Heard, me saluting, than he leaped for joy!"
Then, fill'd with the Spirit of God, she blessed the Maid:—
"To her who could believe, shall be fulfilled
The whole of God's high counsels." And Mary said:—

"My soul rejoiceth in the Lord,
My spirit triumphs in His word;
He looked upon my low estate,
And, looking, made His handmaid great:
To God, my Saviour, be the praise,
Who lowliest men doth highest raise!

"Henceforth the generations shall
Name me for Blessed, one and all;
He that is mighty hath to me
Done great things, low though my degree:
His mercy is for ever sure
While tribes and nations shall endure!

"Holy His name, and full of grace
To them that fear, and seek His face:
His arm with ready strength is found
To cast the high ones to the ground,
Scatter the proud, the meek upraise,
And nourish all their sheltered days:

"The rich go empty, and the poor,
Filled with good things, shall leave His door;
Princes from thrones He putteth down,
To raise those meek who be His own:
To His servant Israel brought He aid,
The promise He of old hath made;—

"That mercy should remembered be,
That Abraham his race should see
Countless as sand on the seashore,
Blessed by their God for evermore!
The promise that hath been of old
To Abraham and his sons foretold,
To kings and prophets dimly shown—
His secret—now, He maketh known:

The promised SEED is come, and I,
Poor Maid, by God, am set on high!"

IX

THE DAYS OF THE VISIT

THREE happy months the Holy Women held—
In field, 'mid lonely hills, on quiet roof—
Sweet converse, of those things the prophets spake
Concerning Shiloh, and him, should go before.
Not yet had Mary shaped her lips to the Name
That is above all names; but in her heart,
"JESUS," she breathed, tremulous with delight
And rosy joy—awful, for amazement wove,
With fear, the weft across her warp of love.

And, many a time, would they to Zacharias
Look for interpretation; who would write,
Being mute, the thing they asked of him; for he
Was learned in the Scriptures, being a priest:
" 'Goeth forth as bridegroom,'—shall Messias wed?"
" 'Meek, sitting upon ass,' is this the King?"
" 'He is led as a lamb to the slaughter '—not my Son!
Nay, holy man of God, this cannot be—
The Ruler of His people shall not die
At the hands of the violent!" And Elizabeth,
"What meaneth 'hills made low and valleys raised'?"

With many questionings came the Holy Women;
And he, the priest, who knew himself full learned,
Astonished at their understanding, owned
Him ignorant before them; but they held
Him wise.
            Not all of themes, awful for woe,
August in dignity and suffering,
Or joyous beyond measure, did the two
Hold converse; but the common tender talk
That mothers use was theirs; and—as they spake

Of breast and milk and little children's pains,
Each could have said she heard a cooing babe.
Thus, for three months: then Mary returned home.

X

THOU DIDST NOT ABHOR THE VIRGIN'S WOMB

WHAT happened to the Maid? Did pointed finger,
Eyes turned aside, bring hot blood to her cheek?
Must the Christ enter through low gate; of shame,
E'en as through gate of shame they drave Him hence,
That none might taste an anguish strange to Him?

"When Thou tookest upon Thee to deliver man,
Thou didst not abhor the Virgin's womb."

Joseph heard rumours; knew his people's law,
But suffered for the Maid betrothed to him:
He would not put her to an open shame—
Was minded privily to put her away
In pity, not in anger; he was just.
And, while he pondered, came an angel down
And spake with him by name, knowing his birth,
Though he a poor man's son and wrought for
bread:—

"Fear not thou, Joseph, son of David's house,
To take thy wife because she hath conceived;
The Child she bears is of the Holy Ghost.
She shall bring forth a Son, and Jesus thou
Shalt name Him, for His people from their sins
He comes to save; thus spake the prophet Esaias:—
'A Virgin shall conceive, and bear a Son,
And they shall call His name Immanuel.' "

These things saw Joseph in his sleep, and rose
To give the shelter of his roof and love
To the sore-grieved Virgin—maiden-wife.

Acquaint with shame ere yet He left the womb,
The King and Saviour of mankind did come!

XI

THE BIRTH OF JOHN BAPTIST

Meanwhile the days of silence were fulfilled
For Zacharias: his wife, Elizabeth,
Bare him the promised son; and all their kin
Rejoiced, for the Lord had magnified
His mercy upon her. The neighbours came
To circumcise the child on the eighth day:
"After his father must the son be called";
And "Zacharias" they would name him; she,
"Not so, but John shall be his name." "Why John?
None of his kindred goeth by that strange name!"
And finding the mother willful, they appealed,
As well they might, to the still speechless sire:
He for his writing-table signed, and wrote
"His name is John": and, marvel, at the word
His mouth was opened, and his tongue unloosed,
He spake, and blessed his God! The friendly folk,
Marveling at all the wonders they had seen;
Knew, with the Patriarch, "God Himself is here,
And we, unknowing!" and when they sought their homes
Among the hills, they whispered here and there

What great things had been done; and all who heard
Laid up an expectation in their hearts—
"What then shall this child be, with whom is God?
No prophet hath risen in Israel for many years!"

And his father, Zacharias, being filled
With the Holy Ghost, prophesied and spake:—

"Bless'd be the Lord, the God Of Israel,
Who hasteth now His promise to fulfil:
Who hath redemption for His people wrought,

Horn of salvation, of our flesh, hath brought –

"A living refuge, come of David's line,
(As spake the prophets, adding each his sign)—
Salvation from our enemies, and all
The foes within that most our souls enthral.

"And to our fathers He doth mercy reach,
Remembering His covenant with each,
The oath that unto Abraham he sware,
That we should serve Him henceforth without fear;
"That righteous, Holy should be all our days,
And all our thoughts converted to His praise!
Thou, should, in this, God's kingdom, hast thy part,
Prophet of the Most High, and herald, art,

"To go before the Lord, and make His ways
Ready, His folk, prepared for His praise;—
Because they known how God salvation brings
And comes to men with healing on His wings,

"The Dayspring from on high, whose gradual light
Shall spread o'er desolate nations of the night;
Shall, shining, bring to captive souls release,
And guide our feet into the way of peace!"

And the child grew; full early was about
His Master's business: no dalliance for him
Within the kindly precincts of his home;
Stress of the Spirit drave him forth to wastes—
Still, silent places, where the voice of God
Could reach him, undisturbed by fret of life,
Through all the years from infancy to man
God taught this, His last prophet, of His ways,
Who lent his ear obedient to the Word:
Might we but know the lessons, day by day

Line upon line, imparted!—He was great;
None greater had arisen in Israel:—
For the rest, he was in deserts till the day
Of his showing: his parents, they who loved him,
Let him be.

XII

THE NATIVITY

IT came to pass, there went out a decree
From Caesar Augustus to enroll the world:
Each one to his own place, the people went.

And Joseph, too, went out of Nazareth,
City of Galilee, to Bethlehem,
King David's city in Judæa, for he

Of David's lineage was; and took with him
Mary, his espoused wife, being great with child
For her, they journeyed slow; and when they reached

Bethlehem, behold, the Khan was full of folk
Who all had come to register their names
And groups sate here and there, and talked and ate.

Now, Mary's hour was come, and she was full
Of anguish, with no place to house her in;
So Joseph, anxious, brought her to the byre

Wherein the travelers' beasts were housed, and there
Found room for her: and, lo, the beasts were still
Nor gave annoy, what time he, careful, made

What poor provision for his wife he might:
Cold was the night and still, when, thus alone,
The mother bare the Son; and none did see
The brightness of His Rising, save the two.

In swathing bands, she in a manger laid,
For shelter from the cold, the princely Child:
Nor knew that there she laid the BREAD OF LIFE

Where ass and oxen for their fodder came.

Not, from His infant birth, the Son of Man
Had where to lay His head in this His world,
But shared the common place the cattle used.

Bless'd Virgin, who didst bear the WORLD'S DELIGHT!
Bless'd Joseph, who first saw the wondrous sight!
Good byre, which sheltered Him from rude affright!
Kind cattle, graced above all beasts that night!

"I was an outcast from my mother's womb."
"While yet I hanged upon my mother's breasts,
Thou wast my hope."
"There was no room for them in the inn."

THE SHEPHERDS AT BETHLEHEM

Now there were shepherd in the field that night,
To watch their flocks; the stillness seemed to them
Portentous, every star an omen: awed
By the silence, they held solemn talk;
Talk of Messias, and the whispered hope
Afloat among the hill-folk—how one John,
A prophet of the Highest, had been born,
And he should go before Messias; how, here,
In Bethlehem, should Christ come; so spake the seer,
And all men knew that here was David's city.
"And shall He, also, be a Shepherd King,
Who knows his folk by face, as we our sheep,
And calls each by his name; who shelter finds,
And pasture, for His flock, and leads them forth?
Ah, might we live to see the promised day!
But who are we? Our place is far apart
From any pomp of kings!"
                                    And as they spake,
Behold, as sudden glory filled the night;
An angel stood beside them; said, "Fear not,
Good tidings of great joy, I bring to you—

To you and to all people; this day is born
To you in David's city, Christ the Lord!"
The shepherds held their peace, nor yet could speak
For joy and consternation; so answered them
The seraph, knowing their thought: "and this the sign
Which shall confirm to you these mighty News—
In swaddling clothes, and in a manger laid,
A Babe shall ye find."—Whereat a multitude
Of the heavenly host now saw they with that one,
And these all sang together, praising God:—

"Glory to God in the Highest, and on earth
Peace and goodwill to men who bear good will!"
And, chanting still that chorus, they went up.

Prostrate upon the ground the shepherds lay,
Trembling with joy and fear: then, "Come," said they,
"Let us go even now to Bethlehem
And see the thing the Lord God hath made known—
That He should send great News to such as we!"

They came with haste, and found the Infant lying
In a manger, as was told them; and with Him
Mary and Joseph; and worshipping, they fell
Before that mystery—Messias, born

A Babe in this poor place, with none to welcome,—
Save only the Sons of God shouting for joy!

Humble before, humbled they went away;
And told their tale to all who cared to hear;—
    "The Christ, in sooth, is come—in such poor state
    As might the child of beggar at the gate;
    But seraph spake with us, and glory shone,
    And multitude of angels joined in song!"
The people marvelled at the shepherds' tidings:
Some talked and soon forgo and some remembered
But Mary kept these sayings in her heart,
Compared with the others times and angel came,
And pondered day by day these mysteries.
The shepherds returned—even as the angels went—
Praising their God for all the wondrous things
Has been vouchsafed to them to see and hear.

XIV

THE0 CHILD CIRCUMCISED AND
PRESENTED IN THE TEMPLE

Now when eight days were passed, the Holy Child,
As bids the Law, was circumcised: no friends
Were hospitably called to this poor feast;
But they named Him Jesus, as the angel bade
Ere yet He was conceived in the womb.
Thus height of grace and death of ignominy
Followed the Holy Child through every stage
Of His yet infant life.

    Acquaint with mortal pain,
      Obedient, borne,
    He suffered in the flesh,
      Of glory shorn.
No lust of flesh that frame should mar
Wherein the Son of Man went forth to war.

The days prescribed for purifying past,
Joseph and Mary brought Him to Jerusalem
To give Him to the Lord: for it is writ
That every first-born man-child shall be His:
Would hints of glory gathering round the Child

Take shape of greatness? Mayhap, God might show
If the Babe they carried were indeed his Son.

Poor folk, these brought the poor man's scanty gift
To symbolise their presentation, doves.
They trod, a peasant pair, the temple courts
Bearing a child; without or circumstance
Or state to show His birth—such group of three
As every day appeared in precincts holy,

None taking heed. This family was observed:
There dwelt in Jerusalem one Simeon,
Who knew: he, righteous and devout, was told
Of the Spirit, he Christ should see in the flesh;
His prayers by day and night, fervent desires
For Israel's Consolation, should be graced.
So sure was he of this, he watched always:
No common, usual group might, unaware,
Pass this man, lest so he should miss the Child:
Perceiving he was ready, the Spirit led
Him straight to the temple; and when the parents came,
The simple peasant folk, behold, he knew—
Such is the gift God granteth to His own,
Through signs of everyday they Him discern—
While haughty scribes and priests, collected there,

Gave scarce a glance to these poor country folk;
A hundred such, sure, came there every day!

Now, reverent and meek, approached the priest
With arms outstretched to hold the Holy child:
Receiving Him, he blessed his god, and said:—

"Now, let thy servant, Lord depart in peace,
        Mine eyes have seen the King!
Thy word to me fulfilled, bid my days cease,
        Which no more joy can bring:

"For thy salvation do mine eyes behold!
        The very Christ of God
Before the face of all the world foretold—
        The King, whose feet are shod

"With gospel Thy peace for all mankind!
        Not for the Jew alone;
The Gentile also shall salvation find,

For He shall make both one.

"To Gentiles, surely, shall the Christ be shown;
His light shall shine on them:
But this glory is for Israel alone—
The Birth in Bethlehem!"

*Out of Zion hath our God appeared
In perfect beauty.*

*He shall rehearse it when He writeth up the people
That He was born there.*

Thus spake the seer, in sacred vision rapt;
Joseph and Mary stood beside, awe-bound,
Marvelling at the great things spoken of Him,
The Child they had brought to the temple: ever more
Glory, greatness, grace, to Him ascribed,
With each new word of God falls on their ear.

And Simeon, looking at the amazed pair,
Blessed them; and to Mary, His mother, said,
          "Behold,
This Child shall be for the fall of many great,
The raising up of lowly souls in Israel;
A sign shall He be many shall speak against,
Perceiving the will of God with rebel hearts

"Yea, and a sword shall pierce through thine own soul!
For He shall suffer, and the smart be thine:
And all the thoughts of men shall be revealed
By the sure witness of the word He speaks."
Mary heard all, and pondered in her heart.

Another graced to hear the News was Anna,
Daughter of Phanuel, of the tribe of Asser,

A widow of a hundred years or more
Who dwelt in cell within the holy precincts,
And day and night was in the temple courts
Fasting and praying. She, like Simeon,
Waited the consolation of Israel.

Stirred anew to hope by inner impulse,
And coming at that very hour to Simeon,
She also saw the Christ and blessed her God.
Many who sought the temple knew full well
The aged prophetess, and to them all
She told how God had visited his people.

The happy, gracious child grew and waxed strong,
Filled with wisdom—as a child may be—
Lovely in all His infant ways, nor marred
By rude offence of wilful humankind:
And the grace of God was upon Him.

XV

The Kings from the East

NOR came the Desire of Nations all unknown,
Save to the two or three in Bethlehem
And Jerusalem to whose eyes He was shown
There in the East—where stars are wonderful,
And men, compelled to gaze at midnight skies,
Therefrom draw omens—in the East were those
Who searched the skies for presage of a Good
Which should be unto all men—Christ of God.

And God, who answereth ever in accord
With our poor prayers, sent to those sages learned
The sign they sought: Behold, His star in the East!
They gat them up, and came in Eastern state—
Perchance, three kings, as ancient fable tells,
For should not kings to His bright Rising come?—
Seeking Jerusalem, where King Herod was
What man so likely as the king to know
Of this new royal Birth: then, "Where is He,"
They ask, "that King of the Jews is born? For we
His star in the East have seen-and come to worship."
Thus spake they to the king, nor feared at all.

Rumour of this strange quest spread through the streets
Jerusalem was moved: with holy joy?
Nay; as the king, the people: fear and dismay
Troubled the peace of the easy-living folk.
Herod dissembled with the kings; would show
Him zealous in their eyes; and, gathering scribes
And chief priests of the people, asked of them
Where the Christ should be born: they answered straight
In Bethlehem of Judæa, thus spake the prophet
Thou, Bethlehem, in land of Judah, art

In nowise least among the princes there,
For out of thee shall come a Governor,
The Shepherd of My people Israel."

Sudden, a murderous thought o'ertook the king
He called the wise men privily, and learned
Of them, with care, what time the star appeared:
"Go," to the sages said he, "search concerning
The Child, and when ye have found Him bring me word
That I may also worship this new King."
Simple, they heard the king and went their way;
When, marvelous! the star that was in the East,
Bright, saw they over where the young Child lay:
Whereat exceeding joy filled their good hearts.
Nor were they moved to find in how poor place
The Child and His mother dwelt; obeisance before
The Holy Child made they—touching the ground
With honoured brows, and, carrying His infant hand
To those same brows, swore fealty, as men
Born in the East life-long allegiance vow.
Spreading their treasures open, they offered gifts
The myrrh of suffering, frankincense of prayer,
And regal gold; for these three men were wise,
And knew how He they worshipped should go forth
To suffer, teach, and pray, to rule—a King.

Well satisfied of heart, elate with hope,
They left, and thought to bring King Herod word:
But that night, as they slept, a counsel came
Return not unto Herod." So they went,
Obedient, to their land another way.
Oh, happy sages come from out the East,
To whom the Christ of God was manifest!

XVI

FLIGHT INTO EGYPT

The Holy Family reposed that night;
But th'angel spoke to Joseph in a dream—
"Flee," the august mandate, "for Herod seeks
The young Child to destroy Him. Go thou hence,
Take child and mother into Egypt; there
Abide till I shall tell thee." And he arose,
Straight, as man under order; waked the mother,
Who, fearful, heard the dream, and snatched the Child
As from peril of death, quick wrapping Him
With mother love for journey. They soon gat
The small gear they must carry, and went forth—
Wanderers and homeless in the night: but, rich
Beyond who dwelt in palaces, they bore
The Saviour of His people Israel.

When poor folk journey, distress attends their way:
We fain would know all pains that Jesus bore,
Tell every pang that magnifies the more
His grace to usward! Otherwise, the mind
Of the Spirit:—"there till the death of Herod"—
This, all the word vouchsafed to love, hungered
For crumb of knowledge of that Blessed Life,
And, "out of Egypt have I called My Son,"
Their warrant for returning—prophet's word.

Of toilsome travel, perils by the way,
Of strangers' lot in Egypt, neglect and want;
Of the first infant graces of the Child—
Concerning these, no word for loving hearts!
Is't true, that painter's vision—how a troop
Of buoyant children upon rainbow wings
Gamboll'd with infant glee round Infant King?—

Those innocent martyrs first to die for Christ!

True? Who can tell! But this, at least, we know—
Their young men shall see visions; old, dream dreams:
And sweet Madonna-pictures, gracing the world,
Fair visions of the Mother and the Child,
With pomegranate, or apple, or with book,
'Mid bowering roses or fair lilies pure,
With infant playmate, or wedding a sweet saint—
All these are true; for, what the sum of them,
But Holy Child on lap of mother pure?—
Such sight the painters saw at many a door.

XVII

Murder of the Innocents, and Return

Meanwhile, King Herod, mocked of the wise men,
And wroth exceeding, made of rage excuse:
He still would have the young Child's life: on all
The little boys, two years and under, death
Decreed he, at the hands of his men-at-arms.
What need of bloody sword 'gainst baby strength
And piteous mothers' wailing?
                          Too small a thing
For History's record, this: any day a score
Might die of infant ailment, and who care,
Save that fond mother who fed eyes on each,
That father of whose flesh and blood each was?
Why not a score of babes, to justify
High policy—remove grave source of peril?
For how would Rome regard this Infant's claims?

Before our God there be no small or great:
Anguish of mothers, blood of clinging babes,
Had, ages before, cried out to the just God:
The prophet Jeremiah told men how—
     "A voice was heard in Ramah,
     Weeping and great mourning,
     Rachel weeping for her children
     And would not be comforted, because they were not."

Good is't to do the will of God and die:
Full ill to hurt and kill and sacrifice,
For ends of ours, bodies and souls of men:
Sins of oppression are not forgot of God.

Now, Herod dead, and angel of the Lord
Appeared in a dream to Joseph; said to him,

"Arise, and take the young Child and His mother,
And unto the land of Israel return,
For they are dead that sought the young Child's life."
Thus, out of Egypt did He call His Son.

Joseph arose; took the young Child and mother,
And journeyed with them back to Israel:
But not in Bethlehem, David's city, stayed;
A new king, Archelaus, Herod's son,
Reigned over Judah—a danger to the Child.
Once more was Joseph warned in a dream:
Obedient, he withdrew to Galilee,
And came and dwelt again in Nazareth,
The fair and careless city he best knew.
Thus was fulfilled the prophet's oracle—
Small honour should his birth place bring to him;—
Called a Nazarene, not Bethlehem-born;
Come out from a mixed people, scorned of Jews,
Not from King David's city—of lineage pure.

So they who sat in darkness saw a Great Light
Running a daily round before their eyes,
E'en as the sun in heaven. And, might it be
Good that the Son of God, in that free place,
Should grow, and all unhindered, manifest
His grace—not trammell'd by continual bond
Of the Law, a burden, laid by man, no man
Could bear? "Suffer the children," He hath said.

XVIII

THE HOLY INFANCY

Many a legend of a princely child
    Brought up in peasant's hut delights the mind;
We like to ponder, how, by manners mild,
    And truth, and princely courage, men might find

A certain clue to the royal alien's birth:
    What then of the meek Son of God, who came
To sojourn as a poor man's child on earth,
    Seeking nor place nor power, nor making claim

On any man's observance? How the hearts
    Of all His Christian people would embrace
Least hint of His sweet living in those parts
    Of Galilee! But there is left no trace

Of how, amongst the children of the place
    He went and came, learned lessons and played games;
How every word and act of childish grace—
    All lovely and unmarred—His Birth proclaims.

In vain we linger o'er the Bible page;
    A few brief words sum up the precious tale:
What if, from other children of like age
    To get knowledge of Child-Jesus we prevail?

As others be, may we conceive the Child,
    Engaging, loving, innocent and gay;
As other children are not, undefiled
    By little selfish end or willful way.

Gracious are other children; but in Him
    All graces gather, lovely, in a flower:

In Him we see, with eyes no longer dim,
    That God to the world gives children, its glad dower.

Each little child reveals some separate grace
    Of Him, the Child that unto us is born:
Christ is discerned in every shining face
    That cheers a home with gladness of the morn.

Men think not of the light; they only see
    Colours and shapes of things; unclean and clean:
So, that "Great Light" that shone in Galilee
    Revealed or good or evil, else unseen.

The Child went in and out; men understood,
    As with enabled sight, perception fine,
How foul all ill: how fair and sweet all good:
    Nor knew the light they saw by was divine.

They loved the Light ere yet the Light they knew;
    Gracious, submissive, affectionate and mild,
In all men's favour day by day He grew;
    A stumbling-block to no man, yet,—the Child.

Men saw, too, all the world in colours new—
    Sun, and green field, and little bird, and flower;
They wondered at the joy of heaven's blue;
    They wondered at the richness of the dower

Their God had newly, so it seemed, bestowed;
    Nor knew that light had fallen on common things;—
Showed jewels scattered by each usual road,
    All men's possessions, rich as those of kings.

The Father sent the Son to be our Light,
    He saw Him shine in His still infant days;
Noted child-wisdom in His ways; delight

In God and man and world; heard His pure praise:—

AND GOD SAID,—

THIS IS MY BELOVED SON, IN
WHOM I AM WELL PLEASED."

BOOK II

THE NOVITIATE

I

JESUS ABOUT HIS FATHER'S BUSINESS

To Jerusalem, year by year, the parents went
To observe their nation's solemn Festival;
Nor knew they took the Paschal Lamb that year—
White, without blemish, set apart to be
Sin-offering before God for all the world!

When he was twelve years old, now, went He up
With all the joyous company, praising God.
There, in the temple, the boy took on Him,
As custom was, His part in Israel's life—
A son of Judah, called for praise of God.
As dim previsions come to our dull minds,
Did He, conditioned as a child of man,
Hear, while He shared the sacrificial Feast,
The echo of a Word—The Lamb that was slain
Ere the foundations of the world were laid?
Did he foresee, scarce knowing what He saw,
The Last sad Supper, when the Lamb of God
Gave of his flesh and blood at dying feast?

The days of the Feast went by; quick-rising thoughts
Surged in the heart of the young Son of Man:
Think what it were, if, all at once, the sun,
Faces of men, service of prayer and praise,
The immanence of God, grew real to thought,
Each with its full significance! The wonder of't
Would send us dazed and faltering on our way:
A child sees somewhat—this Child saw the whole,
All, full of pristine meanings, awful claims;—
Things grow not stale to the Eternal Mind.

Now when His parents returned, the Boy Jesus

Tarried behind them in Jerusalem,
His home, the court of His own Father's house!
The folk returned in two gay companies,
The men and the women, while the children ran
From one to the other as their humour was:
Thus it befell that they had gone a day
Or ever his parents knew the Child astray.
Inquiring among kinsfolk and acquaintance,
They hurried, anxious, up and down the camp
Couched round the evening fires; This mother wept,
Blaming herself for holy trust betrayed;
And every word she treasured in her heart
Revealing the Child's state, returned in chiding.

Back to Jerusalem turned they, seeking Him;
And, for three fevered days of much distress,
The Child they searched for in each likely place;
But not in that where, had they understood,
They first had sought, unanxious and assured.
After three days they found Him in the temple;
Here was the Boy, sitting among the doctors,
Fulfilling all the part of Jewish child
As Moses had conceived it:—"What mean ye
By the lamb, the bitter herbs, loins girt, and sandals
Strapped for journey?" what joy in this young scholar,
So apt to learn, so strenuous to attend
And quick in apprehension! All the tale
Of Israel's great deliverance they told
To the Boy who knew, and fain would know much more
The past was plain, but the great Feast looked on:
His teachers found their settled thought perplexed,
Their knowledge failing, as the Boy's replies
Opened new, simpler meanings; while, unconscious,
He brought fresh thought to bear on time-worn themes,
And showed how their stale words of letter-lore
Looked, quickened by the Spirit. Day of grace

Came to these pedant doctors as they asked,
Aside, questioning each other, "What think ye
Of th' Boy? New wine into old bottles pours He,
And brings Messias to our very door!"—
They, too, were in the Light.
                                    After three days
The parents came upon the group—the doctors
With fervent young Disciple in their midst.
Alas, for Mary! Days of fretful search
Wrought weariness of flesh, soreness of heart:
Blind to His part, she thought but her own
(This once): and His mother said to Him, "Son,
Why dealt thou thus with us? Thy father and I
Have sought thee sorrowing!" even while she spake,
His mother knew her fault, knew she had failed
In love's nice comprehension; she should have known:
"Why is it that ye sought Me?" said her Son,
Wistful and troubled with that life-long grief—
No one would understand! Not one would know!—
But, patient, sweet always, He told her how,
"My Father's business I must be about—
Wist ye not that?" Nor yet they understood.
"My Father"—was the word blissful surprise
To Him who spake—possession realised?
And did the others wonder, taking thought?

We, knowing beyond their knowledge, dimly see
That His Vocation this day reached the Boy:
He heard His Father's call, gave meet reply;
Sate, pupil, in His Father's house and learned,
As meek disciple, at the doctors' feet:
What things are lovely, meet, of good report
In any boy, became the Son of Man;
These, and no other. No subtlety of mind,
No wondrous act miraculous, should mark
The Boy, release Him from the discipline

Proper for growing youths: no "great one" He!
He went down with the two to Nazareth;
Lived there in sweet subjection all the years
'Twixt youth and man's full prime—nor grudged the days.
And wherefore grudge? Is not a single day
With God, His Father, as a thousand years?
Well might He wait until His day should come,
Crowded with all the Life of all the years
Since God made man; of all the purpose, full,
Which God towards man conceived and brought to pass!

II

CHRIST GROWS UP IN GALILEE

And he had much to learn; no royal road
To manhood's slow experience eased his way:
Nor travail of the flesh nor of the mind,
Nor craving of the spirit, ache of heart,
By which boy treads his upward way to man,
Was spared to Him, who needed not that nay
Should tell Him what was in man, for He knew.

No longer ran He freely in and our
The houses of the neighbours, of welcome sure:
The ripening Man saw envy, malice, pride,
May, cruelty, in this house and in that;
And—all His soul oppressed with weight of love
For those who sinned and those they sinned against,
His life all under rule of righteousness—
How could he but displease, and witness bear
Against this man's offence, of that child's wrong?
Stress of the Spirit compelled Him to protest;
Strong contradiction of sinners against Himself
Brought tears of anguish, early agony:
The loveliness and hatefulness of man
Waged their eternal warfare there as here;
And there, in Nazareth, did he strive long years—
Not for Himself—for justice, love and God;
Forbearing, under stripes and strife of tongues,
Through scorn and buffetings, did his patience wax?
In all points tried as we, but without sin!
No harbour of the soul, green place of peace,
Was given the Christ of God wherein to grow.

He knew the poor man's straight and simple thought;
Knew his warm heart, and narrow daily round;

Knew, too, his greed, his superstitions blind;
His family love and sacrifice; dark days,
When hunger sat in the home; his children's plays—
"A wedding now, and now a funeral"
(How kind and gay a playmate found the children
In this young Son of Joseph's house!); He knew
The ache of body, dullness of mind, of him
Who toils for bread: and, as He wrought the wood
At Joseph's bench, did joy in work well done
Flow thence in benediction on all hands
That ply the useful tool, all brains that strive?

Letters, too, learned He, though not in the Schools:
The Scriptures of His people, every jot,
He knew by conning through laborious years,
A patient Scholar—spared no labour here:
And all the wary glosses on the text,
These, too, he knew; how, else, to separate
Wheat from the chaff in the full day to come?
We, His disciples, may conceive in part
How full the joy to find on written page
That very Word whose echoes in His heart
With more distinctness heard He day by day!
With what high filial rapture would He trace
His Father's gradual working towards that end
Now given to him to accomplish! How would grow
Conviction in Him, That He, indeed, the Son,
Come to reveal the Father, His brethren, save!
How would the mountains draw Him ere the dawn
Had flushed their summits, to go forth to God,
And, laying His bared soul before His Father,
Wait dew of promise, of purpose, the strong meat,
To fortify the fragile frame of man—
His flagging mind, his weak unstable heart,
That they the immanence of High God sustain,
He, VERY GOD!

We may not scan those vigils;
We know, as a meek Son, He knelt and prayed:
We know, as son assured of father's wealth,
He made petition that his Father's Will
Should in Him be accomplished. "Lo, I come,
In the volume of the Book it is written of Me,
To do Thy Will, My God; I am content."
And, from the mount descending, how would he
Gather the motions and the modes of things
With quick creative eye, remembering how
(Scarce conscious He remembered), "Let there be"
Had issued from the Word by whom all came;—
The little ant upon her busy way,
The careless singing bird, the glowing flower—
How He would look on these with Artist's eye
As on the finished picture wrought by Him!
A King, He walked the earth,—so meek a King!—
All origins and endings in His hand.

CHRIST, THE POWER OF GOD,
AND THE WISDOM OF GOD

In the beginning of His way
    The Lord Hath possessed Me:
I was set up from everlasting,
    Or ever the earth was:
When as yet there were no depths,
    Even then was I brought forth.
Before the fields, the high places,
    The abounding fountains,
I was there: when He the heavens
    Prepared, and the clouds,
When to the sea He gave decree,
    To the waters, commandment,
Was I by Him, brought up with Him
    I was daily His joy:
Rejoicing alway before Him,
    I went forth in His ways.
With the sons of men My delights were;
    E'en from the beginning,
To earth's habitable places
    I betook me rejoicing.

Wherefore hearken, O ye children,
    As I cry at the gates!
At the coming in at the doors,
    The entering of the city,
Ye simple, understand Wisdom!
    Ye foolish, be ye wise!
Of things excellent, My speech is,
    Things right shall I utter:
I, the Truth, shall speak truly,
    By My Words shall ye know.

Nothing froward, no word perverse
　　Shall proceed from My mouth.
My words are plain to the simple;
　　To him who understandeth
Is My teaching most precious;
　　Receive truth from My lips !
Hear instruction, refuse it not:
　　At My gates watch ye daily;
Who findeth Me, he life findeth,
　　And the favour of God.
Let no man wrong his own soul
　　By the sin against Me.

Better than rubies is Wisdom
　　And knowledge than fine gold.
With Prudence My dwelling is;
　　I, Wisdom, teach knowledge:
When time is ripe for discovery
　　I teach men My Secrets;

Witty inventions then make they,
　　And win praise of all men.
Counsel, too, and sound wisdom
　　Are in the words of My mouth:
I understand all deep matters;
　　I am strong to fulfil
All My orderings, My counsels.
　　By Me kings in peace reign,
And the princes decree justice:
　　The nobles, the judges,
Wise statecraft of Me have learned.
　　Those that ask of Me shall receive,
Those that love Me I love again.
Now therefore hearken, O children,
Seek Him Who for you seeketh!

IV

PREACHING OF JOHN BAPTIST

CHRIST JESUS, Son of the Most High, His gospel,
Beginning at time fixed by several signs:—
Tiberias Caesar's reign in its fifteenth year;
Of Judæa, Pontius Pilate, governor;
Herod, tetrarch of Galilee; his brother
Philip, of the regions of Ituraea;
Caiaphas and Annas, both high priests;—
These things being so, behold, the word of God
Came to that John, the son of Zacharias,
Who dwelt in the wilderness, waiting on Him.

A figure he on whom men's eyes were fixed:
Had they not read the prophets, knew they not
Raiment of camel's hair, and leather belt,
And such spare meat as wilderness might yield?
So all men smote upon their breasts and cried,
"Behold, a prophet of the Lord in Israel!"
And up and down he went, round about Jordan;
His message one, with meanings several
For each soul of the multitudes that heard—
All they of Jerusalem, of Judæa, all
The country, too, and the region about Jordan:—
One word they came to hear: "Repent! Repent!
Repent, that all your sin be put away!
Repent, for the kingdom of heaven is at hand!
Repent, and be ye washed, that ye be clean!"

And as he spake, men bethought them how Esaias
Had cried, "Behold, before Thy face I send
My messenger, who shall prepare Thy way!"
His voice, crying in the wilderness, men hear:—
"Make ready the way! Make ready the way!

66

Make straight His paths: fill up each hollow place;
Mountains and hills being low; make crooked straight,
And all the rough ways smooth, that ye may see,
Ye, and all flesh, the salvation of our God!"
Proud men remembered each his meannesses,
Low men bethought them of their God, and stood
Upright before the heavens; men of crooked ways
Would fain be simple; and the violent man
Grew meek, and washed, and put away his sin.

Men came to Jordan (to the bathing Pool),
And each one told the sin that hurt him most—
The little loathsome sin that spoiled a life—
The hate, the greed, the malice, the pretense,
Mean gains, oppressive ways! But who is this?
The haughty Sadducee, who care for none,
Scoffing alike at penalties and hopes

And present dealings of Almighty God!
What doth he here? He peeps half-furtive round,
To see who sees him,—here be many such!
What power constrains these to the Baptist's feet,
What speech chatters the fabric of their thought,
These godless men of the court? those others, too,
Less conspicuous for soft raiment, arrogant
In piety, broad hem, phylactery,
Features composed to scorn of all the rest,
The common people who know not the law?
By every sign, we know them Pharisees.
Now, will John say soft things to men of repute,
His rugged speech grow courtly these to win?
He scans the crowd with eyes in desert trained
To see from afar; notes these unwonted hearers;
An image form the desert leaps to mind—
From fire of brushwood, how the flames drive forth
The viperous brood, that else had hidden lain—

And straight he hurls it at them; all might hear;
For these the shaft, and these alone it reached:—
"Offspring of vipers, ye, who bade you flee
From God's hot wrath pursuing! What do ye here?
Ye come to be baptized? Go, bring forth fruit
Of Godward turning in your hollow lives!
Children of Abraham are ye? what of that ?
True seed of Abraham walk as Abraham walked
But ye! Nay, of the very stones of the waste
More worthy seed to Abraham shall God raise!
See ye yon hollow tree dead to the core,
With never fruit or leaf to praise its God?
Such tree are ye, and lo, the axe is laid
To your roots! Haste ye, and bring forth good fruit,
Or be hewn down and cast into the flames!"
How received, those great ones of the nation,
The preacher's biting words? Savour of life,
Extracted they, or of death? Nay, none may know.

But the multitude, fear-stricken, beat their breasts;
"What must we do, then? What, then must we do?"
And, all his rigour turned to gentleness,
Straight counsels gave he, apt for simple lives:
"He of you that two coats doth own, let him
Give one to a man that hath none; he that hath bread,
Let him have pity likewise." Moanings ceased
And cries; nor arms waved more, nor hands clenched close;
Escape from the intolerable Wrath,
How simple for these simple! They came and washed;
Baptized of John in Jordan, strong became,
Fearful to sin again against the law—
Another law than that their scribes had taught.
The very publicans took heart of grace;
They, hated of the people, asked of him
"What, master, must we do?" Straight on the place
His finger lays the preacher: "Extort no more,

68

When ye the taxes gather, than the sum
Appointed to be paid: so, make you clean."
The soldiers, men of violence, tarried last,
(Sooth, what had they to do with penitence?)—
Their hardihood prevailing, out they came:—
"And we, good master, what would'st have us do?"
A threefold devoir layeth the preacher here:—
"Ye turbulent, from whom nor goods are safe
Nor life itself, high paid, yet grudging still,
In these things mend your ways: do hurt to none,
Nor take from any wrongfully; let wage,
Fair-earned, content you." Cheered in heart, they came
To John for baptism, no longer chid by fear—
"Place for repentance can rough soldier find?"

In expectation, all the people waited;
The innumerous multitudes that day by day
Thronged to the Jordan pool, by Bethabara,
To hear the Baptist preach; endure the rending
Of old familiar habitudes of soul
That new birth doth entail, the piteous weeping,
Wailing as of the lost; the healing, cleansing,
 Of John's baptism, wherefrom they came out meek
As little children, washed, and of good hope.

But, bitter searching to cast out the unclean,
What was it more than that purifying
Their houses go through for the Paschal Feast?
All leaven is removed, but what of that
Were there no Paschal Lamb to bless the board?
The multitudes, expectant, knew them cleansed
But to make ready: what then of Messias?
A whisper went about of awe and fear—
What if this John himself were very Christ?—
Had he not drawn them as no man could draw,
Had made them turn their backs on shameful things

And get them ready for the kingdom of God!
The murmur grew, and reached the prophet's ear:
How easy for a man to judge himself
As others judge him, by success! Why not
He, as well as another, Christ of God?
How beyond measure God had blessed the words
He spake to the people! Might he be the Sent One?
Not for least moment was the prophet's eye
Dazzled by glamour of his own success:
He, what was he! He gazed beyond himself
Looking for One who was coming: he, too, felt
The throbbing excitation of the people;
And he said to them all, "I indeed baptize
With water to repentance, but there cometh"
(Still hear we not the words, see the rapt gaze
Of the prophet as he spake?)—"there cometh One
After me that is mightier than I,
The latchet of whose shoes I am not worthy
To stoop down and unloose as mean-born slave;
He shall baptize you with the Holy Ghost—
With fire of love and might for righteous living.
He goes as thresher forth with fan in hand;
And as He swings His mighty flail about,
Behold, the chaff flies off in whirling waste,
But grain remains to reward the labouring Thresher;
He gathers, diligent, wheat into garner,
The chaff with fire unquenchable He'll burn!
See, to't, ye light ones, cleansed indeed by water,
But with no weight of purpose, strong resolve."

A new thought took the multitude away,—
Christ is indeed at hand, is come for judgment!—
And each searched heart to find or wheat or chaff.

V

Baptism of Jesus

Now, in those days when all men were baptized
It came to pass that Jesus journeyed forth
From Nazareth of Galilee to the Jordan
Unto John to be baptized of him. But John,
To whom man's face was as an open book,
Saw coming, One, the like of whom before
His eyes had not beheld; of countenance
Unsullied from the womb by passing thought
Unworthy, aspect benign and gracious—
So might all living souls and things of earth
Hang cheerful on His glad beneficence:—
Impression like to these, but more than these,
His quick sense caught; as the august Presence,
With never following or sign of state,
Drew near, the prophet quailed before the light
Of Godhead on his brow, not knowing it.

John would have hindered Him from being baptized—
"It is I have need to be baptized of Thee,
And comest Thou to me?" Jesus, regarding
His forerunner with sweet look (who knew Him not
Save as he had eyes and saw), said, "Suffer it now;
Thus it becometh us all righteousness
To fulfill. That which is good for all, is good
Likewise for Me, for Mine, the life of all."
The he suffered Him. Jesus, being baptized,
Went straightway up from the water, and knelt and prayed.
And, behold, the heavens opened, and John saw
The Spirit of God descending, like a dove
In bodily form, and coming upon him
(John knew the sign which answered all his thought),

And, lo, a Voice out of the heavens spake,
"THIS IS MY SON BELOVED, WHO PLEASETH ME."

VI

JESUS IN THE WILDERNESS

Jesus, being full of the Holy Ghost, returned
From Jordan, and straightway the Spirit driveth
Him forth to the wilderness. For forty days
There was he tempted of Satan, and nothing ate:
And He was with the wild beasts all the nights.

Most men have solemn hours of inward searching,
Dedicate purpose, ere they set themselves
To take up that lifework appointed them;—
How best its tasks fulfil, how 'scape its perils,
How worthily and for God's glory work,
For service of men, too, and their own weal?
All men have chart to study, course mapped out
By other men who journeyed that same way:
Traditions, documents, books, wait on all
Who law or physic or a craftsman's trade
Would follow; these, and the counsels of friends:
No man goeth forth on an unbeaten track.

But this MAN, driven into the wilderness—
Not one had been the way that He must tread;
No common calling of mankind was His;
No waymarks of past travelers showed His path
Through perilous wilderness His calling led Him—
An-hungered, He, for grace and heavenly goodness,
Of wild beasts beset, of Satan hindered:—
Those forty days were as the years to come.
Alone, the winepress trod He: "was there, then,
Nor chart nor compass for His way prepared?
The Scriptures of His people! There was traced,
On hundred luminous sheets, his heavy road.
No man had been His way, nor any should;

No man had done His work, nor any could:
But earthly father sets, plain-writ, the tasks
His son must learn: even so had God the Father,
Throughout the ages, thought upon His Son;
And given to chosen men to write in Book,
A little here, and there a little more,
All guiding precepts that the Christ alone
Should know to follow: vicissitudes had marked
On that untraveled land, unvoyaged sea,
Whereon must go the Saviour of the World.
What He should speak, how minister, how suffer,—
These things the counsels of God had occupied
Ere prophet spake or Moses gave the Law.

Not all unmapped His way, obscure His end,
To the Redeemer in the Wilderness:
Familiar with the guide-book of His course
Through years of labour, studious, purposeful,
It remained to order knowledge, shape His plans:—
How thus, and thus, knowing the people well,
He should begin the work of their salvation;
Teach them to think new thoughts, new ways pursue,
Toward new ends, undreamed of hitherto:
"Behold, I make all new!" His awful word,
And ever, as He thought, the Tempter came;
The Accuser had an ill word for the people;
That Mocker plied Him with, Yea, hath God said?
Evermore, What's the Good? that Hopeless cried—
All his insidious temptings so conveyed
That purest heart might not perceive their guile,
Wisest and meekest, scarce their pride discern.

Was't thus, or otherwise temptation came
To Christ, our Lord, our Life, our one sole Hope?
Scarce dare we ask, or let our reverent thought,
Obtrusive, scan the record, were we not told,—

"In all points He was tempted like as we,
But without sin." Behoves us then to asks,
For soul's instructions, how His temptings came,
Lest like assailing buffet our weak frame.

VII

JESUS IN THE WILDERNESS WITH THE TEMPTER

"The wilderness shall be glad, and the solitary place;
   The desert shall rejoice, its blossoms bringing,
Shall deck itself with flowers as a garment of grace
   To celebrate a bridal with joy and with singing!

"The cedar-trees, the glory of Lebanon, shall be there;
   The excellent forests of Carmel, the roses of Sharon;
All fruitful things the glory of the Lord shall declare,
   All Beauty, the excellency of our God shall make known.

"Lo I come to show the Father, who shall quicken as the sun,
   Shall bring life to dry places as when the rains have
      begun!"

"Aye, the world shall grow goodness as the wilderness, fruits,
   The shining of God quicken, as desert sun calls forth shoots!"

"Ye weak, whose uplifted hands fail, be ye strong!
   Who go tottering in paths of righteousness, take heart!
Have courage, fearful souls, it will not be long
   Till God save from your enemies; the Lord taketh your
      part!"

"The fearful and the slothful, who is it shall save them?
   Let them trust in the Most High, if, indeed, He will have them!"

"In the volume of the Book is writ, the blind eyes shall see;
   To the ears of the deaf shall their hearing be given;
The lame man shall leap, swift as hart shall he flee;
   The tongue of the dumb shall lift praises to heaven."

"The heart of this people is turned away from their God :

His praises shall tarry till the dumb utter word!"

"In the wilderness shall streams break out, waters in desert
   flow;
   Pools with green grass be in the dry places of the jackal;
Springs shall issue in the land where the thirsty people go;
   Of living waters shall they drink and refresh them withal!"

"What hath cool water to do with quenching desire?
   Men shall spurn at their God and choose burning of fire!"

"No more shall men wander as did the tribes of the people;
   A highway shall be there which the simple shall find:
The way of Holiness, it shall be for the clean, howsoe'er
   feeble;
   The wayfaring men, thought fools, shall not err as the
      blind."

"Every man goeth after his own way; rejoiceth in iniquity!
   What to him is that holy way, where the unclean shall not be?"

"No lion shall be there, nor ravenous beast seek his prey;
   Only the redeemed shall walk there, the ransomed shall
      return;
With songs shall they come to sion, go with joy in the Way;
   Gladness is laid up for them; never more shall they
      mourn."

"The flesh pots! the flesh-pots! What be these joys to us?
   Crucify Him! Crucify Him who mocketh us thus!"

VIII

THE THREE LAST TEMPTATIONS

WAS it thus for forty days and forty nights?
We may not know, no measure have to mete
That long Titanic conflict for the race.
Flesh-worn and spirit-weary, each assault
Left our divine Protagonist, all a Man;
Assault o'ertook assault with never pause;
The foe, who wore not flesh, knew no fatigue:
Continual frustrating of wisest orderings,
Continual blasting of green shoots of hope,
Continual searching out new points of approach,
Continual plainings of an o'ertaxed frame—
All to begin again when all was ended,—
This Armageddon fought for human-kind
Outlasted every battle men have fought
Since time began; Out did them all in anguish.
And we, poor souls, who follow, rank and file,
Endure the conflict for our Captain's sake,
Knowing the victory ours, for He hath fought.

Now, when the Forty Days were at an end,
Three cunning last assaults prepared the foe,—
Counting on Weariness to yield the field,
Dullness of Hunger, Exhaustion's little wit
And little strength for conflict. These we know;
These three temptations meet our human case—
The very three that found out Eve in the Garden,
" 'Tis good for food,"—"Yea, hath God said?"
        —"As gods":
Lust of the flesh, and pride, and lust of power,
By these men fall: temptations craftily
Devised to assail these three—how seldom fail!
And do all three come always? Are assaults

Incessant for a period, then a pause?

"See here be stones shaped each like small browned loaf:—
And why not loaves? Thou art the son of God,
And at Thy bidding substance at the first
Took shape and properties: what worthier use
For that Thy hand hath made than feed the Maker?
Command these stones; they shall be bread to sustain
Thy famished flesh!"
                But never for His use
Did Christ command those servants of His eye—
Health, Strength, and Nourishment, Success and Ease,—
"Man shall not live by bread alone," His answer,
"But by each word that issues from God's mouth."
Silenced, the Accuser pondered a new thing:—
"Shall words sustain—mere breath support a life?"
The word, the breath of God, he knew was life;
A spirit, he might gauge this spirit-law.

If not for Himself, for others, sure the Christ,
Brought low by fasting and long conflict, might
Yet succumb, yield the prize of all the world:
"See, from this summit, how the nations spread
Glorious in riches, might, and better wealth
Of teeming human souls; for these Thou carest,
For these wouldst bear all pangs, for these wouldst die:
But wherefore die? How shall thy dying profit?
The people worship triumph, not defeat;
What is't to them that One should die for them
A mean, inglorious death? Nay, live for them;
Take on Thee royal pomp; spread bounties wide
As the sun's light, and cordial as his warmth;
Reign Thou in righteousness and abundant peace
Shall bless the nations, zealous for thy law!
But worship me in this thing, let me guide
The first steps of thy course, Saviour of men.

And well I'll labour to advance thy cause!
For pride of life, success, authority,
And glory of the world, thou knowest right well
To me have been delivered; to whom I will
I give; from whom, withhold; but worship me,
And all these shall be thine—a world to save!"

But never specious lie, fallacious truth,
Distorted yet the vision of the MAN
Not willful and not proud, nor seeking aught
But service of men, unmeasured, infinite;
In obedience, His stronghold; there is a Word
Shall clear illusive mists: "Satan, go hence,"
Jesus answered to him, "for it is written,
Thou shalt worship the Lord thy God; Him only
Shalt thou serve." What room for other service,
Obeisance to the false to attain the true,
A short and easy way to save the world?
This sought not Christ:—"Lo, I am willing," saith He.

One cunning last assault Apollyon made;
He, the proud spirit, knew the ways of pride;
Thought that he knew pride ruled in every breast;
Believed almighty God in very pride
Had cast him, rebel, from high seats of heaven.
Out to be holy city he led Him forth,
Set Him on high on pinnacle of the temple,
That high place whence men ask for signs from God;—
"Thou art the god that answereth our call,
Do Thou this thing that we demand of Thee!"
That place of pride where men would rule, not serve:—
"Compel this people's faith," saith he to Christ,
"Cast Thyself down before the gazing crowd
And reach the ground from giddy height, unharmed,

Unruffled by a hair; for it is writ"

(He, too, the Scriptures knoweth), "He shall give
His angels charge concerning Thee, to guard,
And in their hands to bear Thee up, lest haply
Thou dash thy foot against a stone:—if, sooth,
Thou be the very Son of God! What man
Dare then lift eyelid to oppose Thy work,
Accredited of High God by open sign?"
And Jesus answered, heedless of beguilings,
Nor amending quoted word with "in Thy ways"
(What angel guardianship for run agates?)—
Jesus gave answer straight-aimed at th' offence—
'Tis not for man, not for the Son, to challenge
His God on this or on the other issue,
Man's part to follow way prepared of God.—
And Jesus, answering, said to him, " 'Tis written
Thou shalt not tempt the Lord thy God."

                                              With that,
The Devil had completed all temptations
And departed from Him—*for a season,* mark!
Then, wistful, watching angels came and ministered,
Restored the weary spirit, exhausted frame,
Of that spent Warrior, Captain of God's hosts.

Did angelic paeans fill the heavens once more
For this, the Second Act of our Redemption,
As for the first accomplished in Bethlehem?
The conqueror bore scars, and mortal fear
(For he was mortal) of anguish in resisting,
Through days and weeks, attack upon attack,
Flesh failing, spirit fainting, yet no pause
In urgency of temptation! Our Great High Priest
Learned in the wilderness what men endure
Who resist the devil for dear sake of Christ.
Henceforth, His watchfullest care, His tenderest words
Most pitiful, were for His own when He,
Who knows the spirit's conflicts, saw approach

To disciple, unaware the assailing Devil.

What fragments gather we for our distress?
Apollyon is another, not ourself;
The heart takes courage against foe without:
There is some Word of God which every thrust
Will parry, so, it ne'er be made again:
The conflict is incessant, lasteth long:
The foe our armour trieth at each point:
Watch, must we; he is specious, knowing how
Through avenue of our good to lead his evil:
His temptings have a period, a set time,
When he must raise the siege and hold we out:
Then angels come and minister to us—
Nigh beaten, wearied, sore at every point—
The tender comfortings of God, the cheer
Of brothers who hold up our hands in prayer:
A *vanquished* enemy annoys our march;
A foe to be lightly turned, and knew we how:
Ours but the perils of a foughten field,
But unwary stragglers from the line of march
Are harried by that vigilant enemy.

But He is pitiful to all poor souls:
As tender mother stretches forth her arms
To save her falling infant, so doth He
Our watchful Saviour, stretch out word of help,
And bids us pray,—He who was led of the Spirit
To wilderness to be tempted of the Devil,—
"Our Father, lead us not into temptation!"
Thus far was our salvation there accomplished,
That never feeble soul shall cry aloud—
"Father, deliver me from the Evil One!"
But straightway comes deliverance from that peril.
Knowing right well how weakened frame invites
The inroads of the foe, Christ bids us pray

That we be not an hungered:—"Gives us this day,
And day by day, for every day our bread!"
Oft as we fall, for we shall fall, "Forgive!"
Be these four all His gatherings in the waste?—
Whom we shall worship—"Hallowed be thy name! "
The subjecting of every willful motion
Of restive human heart—"Thy will be done!"
The loyalty begot of conflict sore—
"Thy kingdom come, O God, to me and all men,
The righteous rule we may not disobey!"—
These trophies of that field of Forty Days
He gathers in one sheaf of prayer, "Our Father";
And bids us, "When ye pray, say thus and thus.

Glory to the Father, who hath given the Son,
And to the Son, who for mankind endured
For forty days temptation in the wild;
And to the Spirit, who gives strength to men,
That they may, in their turn, resist the Devil!
                                        AMEN.

1. Of Dreariness.

A SOLITARY place—a heaven of brass,
      Fierce, shining, pitiless:
For thy poor feet no sward of yielding grass.—
O'er rugged ways of iron must thou pass
      In painfullest distress:
The very dews forget their tender power;
A smarting hail of dust, the only shower

And Duty, barren Duty, all around,
      As stones of iron, cold;
And Law, fierce, flawless Law, the dreary bound
That all thy heaven shuts in: nor gourd is found
      Nor stream, nor sheltering fold;
No ease, no hope, no human love to bless
Thy faintings in this hungry wilderness.

But list, a voice,—sure, friendly is the tone,—
      "Nay, hath God set thee here,
And doth He offer for thy meat a stone?
Then is it that He knows thy will alone
      Can bid abundant cheer;
Abjure thy toils, sit soft, and take thine ease,
And, lo, these stones shall feed, this desert please!"

Hence, Charmer, wise as false, who know'st so well
      With truth to trick thy tale!—
These stones in sooth yield meat to holy spell:
"Take thy tasks to thee, selfish aims expel—
      Lo, comfort shall not fail!
Thy choice, as His, to do the Father's will,—
Behold, the Word that bids is Bread to fill!"

2. Of Disappointment.

A SOUL with folded powers
Sits cow'ring close: the hours
Hang heavy on the wing
As birds of night, nor sing
For joy, nor soar in hope,
Nor ask for any scope!
Since yesterday, how long—
As a forgotten song,
Familiar in old days,
Lost "long ago" shall raise,
And yet bring back no part
In the old stir of heart—
E'en thus is yesterday!
So wholly pass'd away!

O how one little cloud
A whole bright heaven may shroud!
How one unkindly smart
Shall desolate the heart!
Life's promise hollow found,
How shifts the solid ground
From 'neath despairing feet!
What solace is there meet
When self stands prob'd and torn
Of love and promise shorn?

The Kingdoms, ah, the Kingdoms!
The glory of the Kingdoms!
A singing Voice shall soothe,
Soft promises shall smooth
Pride's risen crest: behold,
For every brightness fled,
Some gaudier glory shed!
The poor self, stripp'd and scorned,

Stands graciously adorn'd
With beauty, praise, and power,
A very princely dower!
And all shall feel the glow;
Cold friends shall live to know,

To feel as fiery coals
Dropp'd on unloving souls,
The goodness from them cast,
The old love from them pass'd:—
Nay, living yet to bless
Through all unworthiness!—
With constancy divine
To pour a flood benign
Of benefits and graces
On the abashed faces
So coldly turned away
From the sore need of to-day!
O singing Voice, how sweet!
O Comforter discreet,
Who know'st so apt a strain
To charm away the pain,
What guerdon for thee meet,
Thou singing Voice so sweet?
Soul list! Another Word:—
"Trust not all spirits heard
In secret whispering thee,
But try them, whose they be.
They bid *thee* rule, the king
For whom the days shall bring
Their fullness? Trust them not:
There is a sweeter lot:
They name thee master? False are they;
Who lives, lives but to obey.
They bid thee serve? They are of Me,—
Their guiding follow'd well is thee!

3. Of Isolation

ALL POWERS, all passions of a man,
Sure, entered the Almighty's plan
   (If God, indeed, Almighty be),
When first the race He did conceive
And made, and left us to achieve
   Or fail, as nature should decree.

For nature makes one man a saint;
Another, feeble goes and faint,
   And what hath God to do with each?
The strong man will accomplish all
His hand attempts, the weak will fall,
   Whate'er of "grace" the churches teach.

Man stands alone, I say; his fate
Rests with him to improve; abate
   Persistent evils in his blood;
Nourish such gifts as came at birth;
In strength of his own hand, go forth,
   With nought to hope or fear from God.

If otherwise, why then, in fact,
God is accomplice in the act
   Whereby a man may wreck his days.
If from some pinnacle he hurl
Health, fame, and fortune, in a whirl
   Of passion, before the common gaze,—

Why, then, hath God so made the man
That his whole life he ruin can
   By one rash act of reckless shame?
If there be God, and God be good,
Why shields He not His hapless brood
   From vice, disaster, bitter blame?

Why have I senses, lusts, desires,
A heart to hate, mind that inquires,
    And doubts, and asks, Yea, hath God said?
The power in me to err condemns
Whoever gave such power, nor stems
    The ill that follow where I'm led.

Aye, led; doth not my nature lead,
And pride, and power, and lust succeed
    In making me their willing thrall?
If God will have me, let Him save,
Prohibit me that ill I crave,
    Nor give me any chance to fall!

·   ·   ·   ·   ·   ·

Thou poor, proud soul, how ready, thou,
To make escape from God, show how
    The fault is His when thou dost ill!
Were there no evil, where were good?
What praise for progress unwithstood?
    If good compelled man, what of will?

Only those valiant souls who choose
To take the good, the ill refuse,
    Nor pleasures seek, nor pains evade,
Are worthy to follow where He leads,
By waters cool, through flowery meads
    Where innocent voices fill the glade!

Thou cri'st that "nature fixes fate,
No man becomes or good or great,
    Save as his nature makes him strong":
To will is all God asks of thee;
Impulse, strength, scope, he granteth free;

But man must *choose*, or right, or wrong!

Else men were puppets in a play
Moved hither, thither, every way
    Without or strength to strive, or choice;
Perchance for this, the Accuser's hour
To test the souls of men with power:
    For good or evil, is *thy* voice?

IX

JOHN THE BAPTIST AND THE DEPUTATION

JOHN, who had seen the sign of the Anointing,
Bare witness to the people, cried aloud,—
"He is come, that One of whom I said to you,
That He who cometh after is before
Preferred, for He before me was; or e'er
God made the worlds, then was He beside Him.
He is become before me" (well for John Baptist!)
"In all the acts and choosings of my days:
How could I please myself, He, there to please?"

His fulness filleth all things, filleth us;
Grace upon grace He showereth on our days:
The touch of God's continual kindnesses,
The little tender things He doth for each,
With scarce a pause to thank Him in: all these
Are of Him, who but late stood in our midst!
The law was given by Moses: all men know
That labour up the ladder of perfection,
Step gained to-day, and three steps lost tomorrow:
But grace and truth, these by Jesus Christ came;—
Recurrence always of God's loving-kindness;
Insight, the power to see Him as He is,
And, in the strength of truth, to put Him first,
For He is before us—in all, preferred.
No man at any time hath seen High God:
The Son who lay in His bosom hath declared Him,
And this His witness—"full of grace and truth."

Now the rulers of the people heard of John:
The Church at Jerusalem judged that it behoved
To make inquiry, Was he the Coming One?
Credentials of a prophet carried he—

A message, working in the people's hearts;
His dress, his hermit-life, these all, a prophet's:
Nay, might he be in truth the very Christ?
"Anyway, we of the temple should search this thing."
So they sent a deputation to the spot
Where John all day baptized in Jordan, Priests
And Levites from Jerusalem, Pharisees.
As men charged with a mission, straight to the point,
They went: "Who art thou?" John, reading their thought,
Denied not, but confessed, "I am not the Christ."
Still might he prophecy fulfil; they ask,
"Art thou Elias?" remembering how the books
Of the prophets closed with, Behold, I will send
Elijah, the prophet, to you before the coming
Of the great and dreadful day of the Lord. "I am not,"
Said John; for teachers sent from God are slow
To recognise their own significance;
How believe that they were thought of from of old?
One query more from these astute inquirers:—
"Art thou that prophet?"—the prophet like to him,
Who should, like him, lead and command the people,
That Moses spake of. "No," again said John,
Nor paused to ponder if indeed he were
Thus honoured by God's purpose long before.
The baffled questioners became displeased:
What right had he, without call or sanction,
To preach to the people with authority?
"Who art thou, then? What sayest thou of thyself?
That we may answer take to them that sent us!"
John answered by an image, drawn from the East,
Familiar to his hearers, used by the prophets.
When Eastern monarch would on journey go,
His heralds go before, and cry, "Make ready!"
And he, who reaps, or sows, or tills the soil,
Must leave his work, go, labor on the road
The king will travel—filling up the ruts,

Lowering hillocks, making straight the crooked:—

The Baptist tells his mission: not the Christ,—
"I am the voice," saith he, "of one who cries
In wilderness, Make straight the Lord's highway,
As saith Esaias, the prophet."
                                    Each of us
In some sort is a voice, each speaks a name;
By faithful work, true word, we utter—GOD;
Our own poor name, in slipshod work, vain speech.
But otherwise the Baptist! No person, he,
With ends of his own to attain, only a voice
Whose single purpose is to speak one message!
Not lost upon these learned, his allusion,
But, petulant, they ask him, "Why baptize,
If neither Christ, nor Elias, nor yet that prophet?"
John answered them, "I but baptize with water,
As any Rabbi might his following:
But while ye question me, there standeth One,
The KING I come to herald, in your midst."
(Had John that instant seen the gracious Presence,
Returned to Bethabara after many days?)
"Ye know Him not; eyes have ye and see not;
But He it is who commeth after me
And is preferred before me, whose shoe's latchet
I am not worthy to stoop down and loose."
No more of that day know we:—what report
They carried back to the great Sanhedrin,
Or had John speech with Jesus at the Pool.
Had John fulfilled his debt to God and the world
When he proclaimed their King to the waiting Jews?
The morrow found him standing by the Pool,
That baptistery of his, with multitude
Hanging, as always, on his word. Behold,
Drawing majestic towards them, that meek MAN,
Form luminous to him, blank to the rest;

And, as a searchlight thrown on ship at night
Shows up crew, cordage, every separate plank,—
A flash of the Spirit lit up all the past
And all the future for the prophet's eye!
"Behold the Lamb of God!" he cried, and the word
Expounded all the history of the Jews
Since that black night when out of Egypt came they;
Fulfilled the hope of the nation—deliverance
By sacrifice,—and here, the Paschal Lamb!
Did John indeed, interpret his own word,
Momentous, awful, fraught with pain and bliss?

But, more, he saw in this his hour of Vision
A larger hope than Jewish mind yet held—
"That taketh away the sins of all the world!"
"Taketh," with a continual act of taking,
Till all the sin in me, the sin in you,
The black sin in the world that hope dismays,
Shall all be taken away, and "There shall be
No more sin." All this John saw as he beheld
A MAN standing in the midst. Yet once again,
Must John declare the precedence of Christ,
That law of every court—the King goes first:
"First in regard of me," first thought of all
Thoughts harboring in my mind, for whom have I
In heaven but thee? in earth, who shall compare?

Another law of the spirit's subtle life
Was given to John to declare—"He must increase
And I must decrease"—hope of Christian hearts,
That evermore shall Christ be more and more,
And I, unworthy I, be less and less!
In expansion of great moment, John tells how,—
"I knew Him not, but that He should be known
To Israel came I, baptizing with water."

Was it another witnessing, or that same?—
"I beheld the Spirit descend as a dove
From heaven, and it abode on Him: I knew
Him not; but He that sent me to baptize
With water gave this sign to me: 'Even HE
On whom thou seest the Spirit descend
And abide on Him, is He that shall baptize
With the Holy Spirit.' this thing I have seen,
So bear I witness, This the Son of God"!

The Sign of the Dove! What might it mean to John?
He knew the sign of the sun, traversing heaven,
The signs of the former and latter rains,
Knew every leaf inscribed with the name of God;
That all things bore the meanings of the Almighty
For him who knew to discern the seasons' signs.
The dove that returned to Noah, spake it not
The homing instinct of the human soul
That finds no place but in God? That tenderness
Of cooing mate to mate—that mystery
Of the Bridegroom and His Bride—Christ and his Church,
Ineffable in married tenderness?
Abiding love, unruffled gentleness
And quietness and confidence and peace,
And constancy of one who sticketh close,—
These things John saw, for all men see as much.
By the sign of the dove, John knew the Christ:
Even so may we; where Christ is, there the Spirit
Broodeth content, constant in holy glee;—
For, "He baptizeth with the Holy Ghost."

Again, upon the morrow, was John standing,
While two of his disciples talked with him,
At that old tryst of the Pool. He raised his eyes,
And looking upon Jesus as He walked
Toward the place of cleansing, cried aloud,

"Behold the Lamb of God!" And they who heard
That living word believed, and followed Him.
 Nor envy nor disertion's bitter pang
Troubled the prophet's soul, able to see,
"He must, indeed, increase, and I grow less!"

Behold, now, washed with water, with Holy Ghost
Anointed, tempered in temptation's forge,
Proclaimed by herald King before the people,
Witnessed by prophet, very Lamb of God,
Acknowledged of the Father, His own Son
Begotten, in whom fully pleased is He;—
With all these signs now see we Christ go forth,
For Redemption of mankind to energise,
Strivings of sinners against Himself to bear,
To Labours, Passion, Death upon the Cross!

BOOK III

FIRST WORDS AND FIRST WORKS

I

Two follow Christ

THE two who heard John speak left him, amazed,
And followed Jesus. Turning round, He saw.
"What seek ye?" said He,—sword of common speech
For thousand small occasions; sword of the Spirit,
Searching out purpose, judging aimless ways:
"What seek ye?" still His word to thee and me.
The question fell as a rebuke on these;
Why track His steps? In shame faced awkwardness,
"Master, where dwellest Thou?" say they; no words
Save blunt, intrusive query came to them.
("Master, we would know where Thou art," our cry.)
Beholding them, "Come and see," His word.
They went and saw. Had they but told whose house
Sheltered the Christ, the name e'en of the street,
 One other shrine for Christian thought there were!
And they abode with Him that day;—two hours
Christ gave Himself, poured out new wine of life;—
And they knew what they sought. As the sun set,
They came forth shining from the Light of the World!

One of the two was Andrew, gentle saint,
Of the four chosen for they lovèd much:
The other, was he John, the scribe who wrote
The words of life Christ spake to common folk?
But wherefore not a word of all that speech
Jesus held with the two in those two hours?
As lover may not breathe in common air
The words she spake when first he told his love,
Is't that this lover the surpassing sweetness
Disclosed to Him in Christ may not reveal?
Or, somewhere in the world, is, yet, a parchment
On which John wrote those first enthralling words?

II

ANDREW BRINGS SIMON

Together had they drawn the laden net,
Together watched the stars on midnight sea,
The brothers, Andrew and Simon, fishers both;—
Andrew, contemplative, and Simon, bold,
Firm and unstable, passionate and sweet,
Chafing and loving his more steadfast brother;—
Andrew must find him first, his due to hear
Before all others the News should change their life.
Nor simple Andrew's task; how tell to him,
Hasty of speech, in judgment all too quick?
But Andrew knew his brother; told his tale
In fewest words, nor offered evidence,
Save the sure proof of passionate conviction:
"We have found Messiah," saith he. Arrested,
Simon made no question; had not the two
In many a midnight watch talked of the Christ,
How he was due to Israel at this time,
And how when He should come they two would follow?

Not unprepared the brothers; when Simon heard,
He let his brother lead him to the Lord;
And Jesus looked upon him; in that look,
Simon perceived that all in him was known;—
The restless eagerness that found small vent
In fisher's labours; love that scarce could spend
Its wealth on home and kin; nay, Christ saw more;
"Thou are Simon, son of John," He said: "Cephas
Thy name henceforth"; so Peter was he called
The new name given by Him who knows to name
Us all; repose and strength He recognised
In him all men knew as restless, fickle, turned
This way and that by his uneasy soul;

A very Rock of the Church Christ saw in him.
And Peter? Did his eager heart fly home
As doves to their window? He who knows us rules.
Always accessible to those who seek,
Perceiving virtue that none other sees,
Knowing what processes the years have wrought
In each man's nature, what there slumbers still;—
Small wonder men were drawn with cords of a man
To this so winning Lord, aware of each!
Three followed him already—fishers all.

III

PHILIP AND NATHANAEL

"On the morrow," the fourth recorded day—
How well we mark the first days of our stay
In a new home, new country! John does more,
New life he chronicles from hour to hour,
Unfolds his memories of fourscore years,
Fresh, vivid, as what passed but yesterday!

Christ went not to Jerusalem, where the scribes
Who knew the law might give a prophet hearing:
A Galilean was He reared; the three
Who followed Him were also Galileans;
Wherefore it was that many works were wrought
In Galilee of the Galileans—link between
The wider world He came to save and Judah.

On the morrow He was minded to go forth
Into Galilee, and there He findeth Philip.
"Follow Me," said the Master, and he followed.
(We bid those only who must obey our word.)
Was it that Philip had so read the prophets
That he knew the Christ when he saw Him?
Happy those comrades of Bethsaida,
Knit long ago by converse of Messias,
Andrew and Peter, Philip and another!

Philip goes forth to find Nathanael—
Subtle and simple, learned in the law;—
"We have found Him, O Nathanael, of whom wrote
Both Moses and the prophets; scorn not thou,
Jesus of Nazareth, the son of Joseph!"
(Messias, out of Nazareth, out of Joseph?)
"Can a good thing come out of Nazareth?"

Nathanael asked with Jewish scholar's pride.
"Come thou and see," was all that Phillip said,
But in the word such strong assurance spake,
The other needs must follow.
                              Jesus saw
Nathanael coming to Him, saith of him;
(Sword of the Spirit, piercing the man's marrow!)—
"Behold, an Israelite in whom no guile!"
Not word of searching praise, how just soe'er,
Should win Nathanael: "Whence knowest Thou me?"
Dubious, he asks; and Jesus,—"Ere Philip called
Thee to Me, I saw thee under the tree."
So simple words! But, as a keen-edged sword,
They pierced the heart of this deep-learnèd Jew;
In solemn words he spake first one more creed
Pronounced in Christendom: "Thou Son of God,
Rabbi, art Thou; the King of Israel!"
Whence knew Nathanael thing that many souls
Seek after all their days nor ever find?
Was it that, underneath the fig-tree, he
Had first cried out to his God, "Haste Thou the Coming
Of Him who shall redeem His Israel?"

Answered the Lord, "Because I said to thee
I saw thee underneath the tree, believest?
Thou shall see greater things than these. That ladder
Jacob once saw where angels came and went—
That sign shall be fulfilled before your eyes;
Ye shall see heaven opened and the angels
Coming and going, on the Son of Man,—
That Ladder, scaling up from earth to heaven,
Whereby men's prayers ascend, God's graces come."

IV

THE MARRIAGE IN CANA

IN CANA was a marriage made;
The bridegroom to the wedding bade
Jesus, His mother, and the five.
We learn not how the guests arrive,
Nor who in the high places sate,
Nor if five virgins came too late:
Nor know we that a single one
Had not a wedding garment on.
We know that Christ was bidden, went,
With royal courtesy of consent:
And every wedding shines in grace
Of that to which He lent His face!

Perhaps for days the wedding feast
Had progressed; all, the first and least,
Were graced as guests with meats and wine,
Observance, service, every sign
That in the hospitable East
Is due from him who makes a feast.
Mary, the mother, seemed at home;
Was it, perhaps, a kinsman, whom
To honour all the guests had come?
 Troubled she learns, "The wine has failed!"
Dismay in all the house prevailed:
But Mary, "What if now the hour
When He shall manifest His power?"
"They have no wine," she told her Son,
Nor ventured what she would have done.

The moment to our Lord seemed meet
To teach for aye his mother sweet—
The days of His subjection o'er—

She might not try to rule Him more:
For no son is it good to be
Guided in his maturity;
And for men's sake Christ spake a word,
Sure not austere when first 'twas heard,—
So never more should grievous thought,
To Virgin Mother's breast be brought—
"What have I now to do with Thee?"
Thy Son, a man, must needs go free
From mother's importunity!

And Mary understood the word:
Nor vexed, nor sore, all undeterred,
She bade the men (as in command)
Receive their orders at His hand.
"Do whatsoever He shall say!"
Alert, they waited to obey.

Six waterpots of stone were set,
Prodigious, so there should be no let
To goodly custom of the Jews,
Their hands, their cups, oft to suffuse
With water while the feast progressed.
His time now come to manifest
By first great sign His power to men—
Ages and moments in His ken
Are all as one, but every deed
Shall, in its time, from Him proceed;
Who hasteth not nor ever rests
Times, by occasion, His behests—
His time now come to show to man
Act of creation once again,
Show year-long processes contract
To compass of an instant's act,
Ripe vintage of the grape flow forth
Without, or seed, or sun, or earth,

And water leave the jars as wine,
With Life informed, of Life the sign.—

"Fill ye the waterpots," He bade;
The eager servants quick obeyed
And filled them to the very brim.
"And now draw out and bear to him
Who rules the feast."—With curious eye
He spake to bridegroom standing by,—
"Most men at first produce their best;
When men have drunk, they serve the rest,
The weaker, poorer sort; but thou
Hast kept the best wine until now!
The bridegroom heard as pleasant jest,
Not knowing that indeed the best
Wine ever quaffed at wedding feast
Was served that day to last and least.
Nor knew the ruler the strange tale
Of what had happ'd lest wine should fail;
Only the servants knew, and they,
For bridegroom's honour, would not say.

As on accession of a king
His servants free libations bring,—
So these, unknowing, graced the Unknown,
The King that day come into His own!

"But to what purpose was this waste?"
The thrifty soul cries in his haste;
"For royal banquet was excuse,
But tuns of wine *here*—for abuse!"

Later, a hundred years, one day
An honoured guest had come to stay:
"You like the wine? You have not met
Vintage so delicate as yet?

Dearer than heart's blood is each drop
To us of this household! Nay, stop
And hear the tale: a wedding here,
My great-great-grandsire's nuptial cheer,
Was graced within these very walls
By presence of the Lord! That calls
The blood to your cheek!"—Then all the tale
He told of how the wine did fail,
How Christ turned water into wine,
More costly, but not more divine
In origin than water is;
And how this wine, a cup of bliss,
Was given to such as love the Lord;
Was offered, too, to those who heard
For the first time of Christ, His power,
And served and loved Him from that hour.
"Cup of communion, do we call
This cup which moves Christ's life in all."

(Who knows but some such simple tale
Our royal Master's lavish vale
Might justify to careful soul
Who nicely calculates his dole?)

V

DOST THOU BELIEVE?

WE linger fondly o'er that gracious feast
Venetian painter portrays,—how gay guests
Hold breath, amazed, at wonder has been wrought!
So would we have it for our Master's praise!
But pomp and circumstance attend not signs
That witness Christ; not wonders these, nor portents,
But signs to challenge who has eyes to see.
Sign, leading thought to that thing signified,
The glory of Christ, was wrought in Galilee,
No man perceiving, only the disciples;
And they, at the first sign He gave, believed;
They saw His glory manifest that day!
Who but Messias would such bounties pour?
Who else could subvert Nature's usual ways?

Not proof that Christ wrought with us all those signs,
(For confirmation of an earlier faith),
But proof of fitness, challenge on the threshold,
To him would tread the Christian's difficult way:
"Behold a mystery! Canst thou believe
That water, at the word of Christ was wine?"
"Nay, but," thou sayest, "I know that Christ was good—
There is none other by whom men are saved;
But why these miracles, magician's wonders,
Unworthy Him in whose hand are our souls?"

"Dost thou believe that Christ wrought many signs,
Made dumb to speak, the blind receive their sight,
The lame to leap, and for the poor poured forth
The treasures of His wisdom?"
                              "I believe!"
To-day must catechumen sure respond:

Else what else is left? A holy man of God,
The great exemplar of our halting lives?
Aye, but how follow? Birds show how to cleave
The air with rapid wing, but can we so?
"But Christ doth more," you say; "He *is* the Way
He shows; we walk in Him; and when we fall,
We cry on Him for help, and go secure!"

Why, here is a miracle, more potent, subtle,
Than water turned to wine, or sudden lull
Of that tempestuous sea! "Whether is easier,"
Saith Christ, "to say Thy sins forgiven thee,
Or say, Arise and walk?" Lo, here the test
For measuring miracles! The easier sign,

Arresting 'Nature's Law,' we stumble at,
Yet pray, "Give us this day our daily bread!"
"Forgive us our debts as we forgive our debtors!"
O fools and slow of heart! The harder thing
We glibly take on trust: but 'Natural Law'
Must needs, we say, proceed in its due course!
Blind that we are, what meaning have our words?
We note a process, and we call it Law;
Yet not one law that guides the universe—
The law by which a leaf takes shape, a worm
Erects those spades of his to dig his way,—
Not the least law by which the worlds consist
Is manifest to men; all's mystery!
Only in Christ no mystery we allow,—
He shall nor do nor be more than man can,
Else we will none of Him!
                           Yet there be tests
Whereby to try each several miracle
Is it indeed of Christ? Not baby play
Of measuring ocean with a spoon to say,
Water, how much; nor meting out His works

By our infantine lore of natural law:
But, Doth each sign we read of show His glory?—
Not pomp of power, splendor of attribute,—
His glory is His Goodness! Let but show
For man such value as counts nought of things—
Simplicity and courtesy and kindness,
Fitness for the occasion, apt response
To need that claimed the act,—by these we know

Whether here be of Christ a very sign!
As naturalist from some small bone constructs
In his thought the mighty mammoth, so each sign
Whereby Christ manifests Himself implies
The whole, and we behold His glory, full
Of grace and truth!

"Our Master, give us grace to read thy sign,
Nor stumble o'er that water turned to wine,
Which, on the threshold of that door Thou art,
Obstructs; lest we too lightly choose our part,
And when temptation cometh fall away,
Nor garner any fruit on harvest day!"

An old man, having slept a hundred years,
Wakes up; what age of miracles appears
The world to have o'ertaken! By magic art,
Each speaks to each, a thousand leagues apart!
Nay, tones are caught and kept a thousand years,
And men long dead shall speak as to their peers!
Shall he go to sleep another century,
In miracle for him, no mystery!
So had the world advanced to understand
How slight a thing 'tis matter to command,
Compared with that high mastery of their mind,
Compels, perforce, th'allegiance of mankind!

VI

A LITTLE GROUP WENT TO CAPERNAUM

A LITTLE group went to Capernaum,
Radiant in glow of an unspoken hope,—
The glory of a kingdom not revealed,—
Jesus, His mother, His brethren, and the five:
Note how they hang behind and tell the signs
Whereby they know Messias in their midst!
How beg again from Mary's lips the tale
Of marvelous Birth, confirmed by heavenly signs;—
His brethren seeing, as ne'er saw they yet,
In Him in their midst a Great One sent from God!
Jesus, reading all their thoughts, knew, as they went,
The loneliness their craving hopes imposed
On Him, the Separate One, offered alway!
Simon, graced with a new name, we may believe
Had leave to lead the band to his own house,
And lay his little wealth before his King,

Not many days abode they in Capernaum.

VII

SIGN OF THE CLEANSING OF THE TEMPLE

Since His twelfth year, He year by year went up
To the temple with his kinsfolk. But this year
The Lord of the temple to His Temple came,
Messias before men to manifest!

And, worthy of Messias, sure, a pile
More vast, magnificent, costly in detail
Of marble. gold, rare stone and carvenwork
Than any building earth sustains to-day!

Little knew Herod he had raised a palace
Greater than that of Solomon;—for why?
Greater than Solomon should go in and out,
Should teach and heal within these holy precincts,
Should there first utter words, sounding to-day
To His kingdom's utmost verge, words of our life!
The King had come to the house prepared for Him
Of His Father, through Herod's liberal care—
Unworthy he to know grace laid on him!

All that vast reach of cloisters, hemming in
The outer court of the temple, searched His eye;
Corinthian pillars, white, innumerous,
Of purest marble, delicately wrought,
Of height surpassing and majestic grace,
Reaching toward the heavens,—fitting were these
For His Father's house, made ready for the Son.

But what of them who occupied their business
In those fair chambers? The Lord of the house hath come:
What meaneth then that lowing in His ears,
Lowing of cattle, innocent cry of lambs,

Cooing of turtle doves in sacred place,
And, worse offense, that clink of many coins
Changed at the dealer's tables? HE is come
That should come! Scourge of small cords He grasps,
And this slight weapon, plied with burning zeal,
Sufficeth all the horde to drive before Him:—
The lusty butcher used to handle beasts
Immense and furious, money-changers' greed
Stronger than ten strong men,—of what avail
That any should resist the arm of God
Wielding His lightest weapon? Forth they go,
An ignominious crew, nor dare to seize
On coin or beast of all their greedy store:
One Man drove forth the money-getting crowd,
Their beasts and they quailing before the Judge!
And John, who saw all, held the sight in his heart,
And knew thenceforth, Wrath of the Lamb, how dread!

"Make not my Father's house a house of sales!"
Cried He whose house it was. And all at once
The disciples bethought them of that word of prophet,
"The zeal of thine house shall eat me up!" and knew
With sudden rapture, sign of the Messiah!
Scared in their pride, the Jews, the priests stand by;
They see a sign, they know it for a sign,
But have not grace of truth sign to receive.
As cobwebs swept He specious pleas aside:
' 'Tis well that beasts for sacrifice be close
At hand, lest the peoples' zeal to offer cool;'
'They come from far, here let them change the coins
They bring, for pieces meet for temple dues:'
'Why hinder we the ignorant, hither come
To do God service?' None of this they plead;
Christ's word about a place of merchandise
Had found them out; they, too, were traffickers,
And knew the rebuke for them; not for naught

Had they afforded all these stalls to merchants!
Swift to the mark goes every word of His,
And, cowed, they ask for sign that they might know
By what authority He did these things.

"A sign?" saith He: "Destroy ye this fair temple,
In three days I will raise it up again!"
They, hearing, understood not; how could they
Receive that doctrine of the holy place
God made in each man for His habitation?
"Full six and forty years," they said, "this temple
Was building! Wilt thou raise it in three days?"
But of the temple of His body spake He:
When on the third day He raised Him from the dead,
The Eleven remembered how He said this thing,
And all the more believed and knew the truth.

Men say, "Now love we but our fellow-men,
And all the secret know we of Christ's grace;
A passion moved Him, all-consuming love
For the weak and helpless, pity for the lost:
Let us but burn with passion for suffering men,
And so are we disciples of the Christ,
Name we His Name, or not, as pleaseth us!"
But, as through same gray skies breaks sudden light
And glorifies a space the common earth,
So through the dull complexion of the days
He walked with men as Man, sudden brake forth
A glory—the master-passion of our Master!—
"My Father's business" and "My Father's house,"
"My Father worketh hitherto," and, "I
And my Father are one,"— as when cloak blown
Aside by wind reveals rich garb beneath,
Such glimpse get we, through words He spoke by times,
Of passion serene, enthusiasm meek,
Ideal, burning zeal, in heart of Christ:

"My Father,"—lo, fresh spring of all His days!
Sole Origin and End of all His ways;
And for His Father's love of men He died!
"But He, too, loves us?" Yea, verily, for He
And the Father, One! How should He save us else?

VIII

MANY BELIEVED

MANY believed, of the people in Jerusalem
During the days of the feast. They saw the signs,
(What others were there done we know not of?
That sign of cleansing, only, we are told)—
Perceived them to be signs, and read aright
The tokens of Messiah. Was He not glad?
Till now but five, now many men believe;
(Our heart is lightened for the Son of Man!)
But Jesus did not trust Himself to these;
All men were to Him as an open page;
He knew the hidden thought of every heart,
(As we may know, keep we the single eye),
And these believed because they saw the signs
As evidential proofs of Him God sent;
But strangers yet were they to all that glory
Of His goodness and humility and love!
What profit in a faith of the mind alone,
That reacheth not the springs of love in a man?

IX

WHAT THINK YE OF CHRIST?

ALL men, of faith and unfaith, ask to-day,
Not knowing that they ask it, What think ye
Of Christ? They question miracles, the Word
As we have received it, a hundred points,
Disputable for the uneasy mind!
A deeper-seated doubt remains behind,
Doubt vital to the happiness of the hour,
To hope for future, forgiveness for the past:—
Is it that Christ indeed can change a man,
His poor, mean thoughts, his selfish, worldly ways,
All that abases him when, in the night,
Of sleep forsaken, vision he abhors,
His own false, worthless, most despisèd self
Persistently confronts him? Can Christ indeed
Change such an one, take from him all his sin,
And all his odious nature, prompt to sin,
Give him instead the meekness of a child?
This the one question that concerns mankind,
As physician with specific should concern
A city plague-struck!
              Having determined,
By that first sign, His power o'er things that show,
(The servants of His hand, fulfilling His word),
Thus early in His ministry He solves
That other painful problem of the soul:
How can a man another man become—
New thoughts, new works, new loves, new fears, new
    hopes,—
And leave himself, the man he hateth most,
As reptile casts its slough, and goes renewed?
The things within the haunted soul of man
Are His to order also. There's no place

Within a man, without a man, within
Some other he would reach, but Christ rules all
For them would have His rule! Herein, our hope.

Was held a council of the Sanhedrin
To discuss this Rabbi, doing many signs?
Did they commission one to go by night,
(So none would see a ruler of the people
Hold equal converse with an interloper),
And sound by subtle questionings His learning?

X

NICODEMUS AND THE NEW BIRTH

HOW good to know that house where Nicodemus
Found the Lord in the night! Had pious soul
Bidden Him occupy a prophet's chamber?
We please ourselves with picture of the scene:—
How, late at night, a cautious knock was heard,
And he admitted to the Master's presence;
How slender wick in oil obscured the room,
But lit up that one Face of all the world,
That figure, seated in tranquility—
A King gave audience in that upper room!—
How Nicodemus sat in the obscure,
And took, unknowing, cognisance of Him
Before whom the world is judged! So may we dream:
We know that courteous, Nicodemus spake,
And frank, as one convinced on certain points,—
"Rabbi, Thou art a teacher come from God,
We know, how else were done the works we see?
No man can do these signs save God be with him."
Thus, friendly, opened midnight conference:
Nor spake the ruler for himself alone;
"We know," his word, including those who sent him.
The mournful interest of occasion lost,
Belongs it to those rulers of the people?
Was this the moment of the open mind
When they, too, had been saved had they so willed?

And Jesus answered, filling that hiatus
'Twixt spoken word and the unspoken thought,
So baffles the poor speech of man with man:
He knew what image blinded this man's heart—
Messias, come to rule, a King, defiant,
Before whom Roman legions flee as the chaff!—

"Hast thou, then, with Messiah aught to do?
Art sent, a prophet, to foretell His coming?"
Such unspoke questions, knowing, Jesus answered:—
"Thou wouldst know of the kingdom, but I tell thee,
No man can see the kingdom, be it come,
Save he be born again. God's kingdom comes
With signs thou wot'st not of: with observation
Come kingdoms of the earth; magnificence
Of kings takes every eye. The kingdom of God
No man can see, but has been born anew:
For such as thou, there shall be nought to see."

The ruler, baffled, vexed, scoffs out reply:—
"What talk is this—a grown man born again!
Again to enter in his mother's womb,
Come forth a babe once more, all life forgot,
All habits thoughts, controlling circumstance?
Such talk flies wide of possibility,
And shows Thou know'st not life, the ways of men!"
(Is't possible, we ask to-day, to change
A man from all he was born and has become?)
The Lord repeats His word, but adds thereto.

"In truth, in very truth, I say to thee,
Except a man, of water and the Spirit,
Be born again, he cannot enter in.
Here be the only means to that new birth
Whereby a man can come into the kingdom."

Water, the ruler knew, for every Rabbi,
Whose teaching differed by a jot form the rest,
Baptized his following. Why not this Jesus?
But the Spirit—that means power—here, a new thing!
Nor testing of the power without the sign;
(Sign, and thing signified, He joins together);
Outward profession, first, for such as he,

Who came to Christ by night, ere any power!

"What is this that he saith—Born of the Spirit?
I know not what he saith!" the puzzled man,
Not baffled by the word, but by the truth
Come on him unprepared, said in his heart;
To whom Christ gave, as His wont, a principle
To guide him through a thousand intricate ways;
To guide us through that conflict of our age,—
Shall *one* law govern matter, govern mind?
"Nothing I see," the man of science cries,
"Which makes me apprehend Power you name God!"
"Nay," saith the Master, "thou hast spoken truth;
Nothing thou seest reveals to thee the kingdom;
To see that must thou new birth undergo;
Born of water and the Spirit, shalt thou see!
That which is born of flesh, no more than flesh;
Spirit is born of Spirit, and hath vision.
Then marvel not that who is born of woman
Discern not mysteries of that other world,
The world of the Spirit; lo, two kingdoms these,
With each its several law! Wouldst keep within
Dominion of the flesh? It is enough,
That what he see and prove a man believe.
Wouldst enter that dominion of the Spirit
Which is God's kingdom? Ye must be born anew.
'Where find this realm, suppose a man would enter?'
Thou wouldst ask; nay, none may track the way
The Spirit takes to reach the heart of man
To whom He brings new birth; free as the wind,
That bloweth where it listeth, is that Wind,
That breath of God, engender the new life;
Thou knoweth not whence it comes, nor whither goes;

Its voice thou hear'st,—The moaning cry of souls,
Distressed, as trees in the wind, crying for God!

That, when thou hear'st it, know the voice of the Spirit;
But think not thou to measure what He doth
By rule that metes out things of sight and touch;
There be two kingdoms with two several laws,
Both of the Father, governed by His word;
But law of the one ruleth not things of the other."

And "Marvel not at this," saith Christ; to-day,
Hint of the mystery transpires to our searching:—
A man conceives a pure love for a maid,
Or notes a new star in the firmament,
Or thinks to traverse space some untried way;—
What has he now to do with things of flesh?
His greed, his lust, fall from him as a slough;
All thoughts revolve round that engrossing thought;
The tissues of his mortal brain take shape
From thought that run among them, none know how;
Behold, a new man, new thoughts, new hopes, desires!—
A man may oft lay finger on the place
Where new thought seized him, made him painter, poet.

So God hath made us, that for every man
Are many chances of being born anew
 Into a life still higher than the first:
What if were one great chance for every soul
Of highest birth creature of dust may know?
What if were some amazing thought, compelling,
That no man could pass by were it once brought
Within the focus of this narrowed vision;
A thought for wise and foolish, vile and pure,
That sudden, certain, should transform a man,
Give him new birth, within an air unbreathed
In all his groveling days! Why, here, a lever,
With arm to lift the world to higher plane!
To make this weary, travel-stained, poor Earth
A place for angels to go to and fro,

A paradise of God!
                    With Nicodemus,
What hath all this to do? Practical man,
He knew and paid all dues of his religion,
All tithes of mint and anise, ceremonious rites:
What was all this, of rustling in the heart
Stirr'd by the breath of the Lord and Giver of Life?
No word of Christ's has penetrated him,
Good honest man, but dense to things of the Spirit;
"How then can these things be? What meanest thou
By talk of wind, the Spirit, some new birth?"
Christ labours not to make His meaning plain,
Already put in simplest speech. He chides
Him rather. "Art thou a teacher in Israel
And understandest not? What teaches thou?
Of prophets, moved by Holy Ghost to speak?
Of mighty men, on whom the Spirit came,
Raised to deliver Israel? Perceivest not,
That I but tell thee of these self-same things?
Verily, verily, is My word to thee,
We speak that we do know; that we have seen,
We testify and tell of; as for you,
This is your condemnation, ye receive
Not the truth when ye hear it."
                              "We" and "ye"—
Here, first, in the history of the yet infant Church,
Appears the dividing line that separates
The world, so multitudinous, so strong and wise,
From that poor two or three gathered in His Name;
The Church, grown great, is known by the same sign
Her Lord announced of her in infancy;—
She, through whatever mark she would impose
In pride of separate life, is known by this:—
She discerneth things of the Spirit, as at first.
The world, how sensible, righteous soe'er,
Calls still, with Nicodemus, "Foolishness,"

The spiritual things a plain man would away with!

Again, that "Teacher come from God," his very words,
Would teach the ruler: "I tell you earthly things,
Of wind and the Spirit, and that new birth takes place
Before your eyes on any common day:
What if I were to speak of heavenly things!"
And, lo, that man caught up to the seventh heaven,
Who saw there things not lawful to be uttered—
For none could comprehend speech of those things,—
Helps the dim searching soul, with single eye,
To range that vista of the heavenly things!
"But no man hath ascended into heaven,
None knows the length and breadth, the depth and height
Of riches unsearchable that be in God,
Save He, the Son of Man, From heaven descended,
Who, walking here with men, abides in heaven."
And now to Nicodemus, slow of heart,
(Never the Son of Man chooseth His hearers,
Recipients of those pearls that be His words!)
To that dull Nicodemus tells He out
That secret the old earth had travailed with
Through many ages, now, to bring to birth!
That secret of the spell should lift the world,
Nor fail in power to raise one soul of man!
"Thou knowest how Moses lifted up the serpent,
And every dying wretch who looked was healed?
So must the Son of Man be lifted up:
All men shall look on Him; and whoso looks,
Seeing the Son with eye that comprehends,
And knowing Him, believes, is born again,
(This, the new birth I told thee of but now),
And is, in Him, eternally alive!"
"Aye, lifted up," murmured the vexed ruler
In his heart, below his light word of farewell;
"He means the throne of Israel, but there is, methinks,

Another way of lifting the presumptuous—
An eminence all men shall curse, not praise!"
And Nicodemus went into the night:
But ever, he being honest, in his heart
Echoed the words he could not comprehend—
"Ye must be born again," "I, lifted up!"

XI

JOHN, LOVING SCRIBE, TAKES UP THE PARABLE

Lest we, like Nicodemus, go forth in the dark,
Nor comprehend that sign of the lifting up,
Nor the mystery of new birth, where from a man,
All staled and hardened in the world's old ways,
Comes forth a tender soul, soon grieved with sin,
Lively and quick in frank pursuit of joy,
And all his joy is, God in Christ who died—
Lest we let this dear tale, like water, slip
Through careless fingers dallying with the deep,
John, loving scribe, takes up the parable:—

For God so loved the sinful world, He gave,
As one gives his best friend a gift of price,
God gave His own begotten Son! Who loves,
Or son, or friend, or wife, or child, he knows
Whether were harder to give his own life,
To suffer pains in himself than in that one,
The very light of his eyes, joy of his days,
Whose hurt he feels with thrice-repeated pang!
God gave his Son to the world—ah, gift supreme!
Would no less gift have served for us, poor souls?
God gave His Son, that whosoe'er believes
On him should have eternal life, e'en now,
Nor ever perish as a soul that dies;
He cannot die, for he is born anew
Into that life, fed by eternal springs,
That knows no lasting languors, horrid drought!
But the glad wretch, reprieved from perishing,
Must do his part; he must believe in the Son.
And this is why none other way was found
By God Almighty than to give his Son,
That men might see Him walk the earth as man,

Knowing how hard it is, in lowly ways,
To keep unspotted of the world, and give,
By word and look and mien, by thousand acts
Of pitiful tenderness, dear life for men!
Hearing such words as man ne'er spake before,
Seeing such deeds as never had been done,
How choose men but believe in such a friend?
And how believing, fail to enter in
Kingdom of God, where love is, and no hate?

Not as a judge He came; not now was sent
To judge the world for all its evils wrought
In the eye of day. Only to save He came,
Through that new infancy of tender souls
Which comes to them who look upon His face.
But judgment is come with Him, howe'er meek
The Son of Man walk among men. Each soul
Judges himself, unknowing; doth he believe?
Then is his judgment passed; he's born again.
Doth he in willful pride still ask a sign,
Rejecting every sign of that sweet Life?
So, too, he's judged; he goes his way, untouched
By the dear grace of God should give him life;
And day by day all soft and tender thoughts
All ways of sweetness, die from out his life;
He perisheth, the while he lives his days.
To see the light, and not to choose the light,—
For light reproveth deeds that love the dark—
What greater condemnation is for men!
Each man, arraigned before his own sure bar,
Goes out to his deserts, or light or darkness.

XII

JESUS AND THE DISCIPLES OF JOHN

Out of the city, into the country parts
Of Judah, came the Lord with His disciples,
To rest awhile after that arduous week
In Jerusalem; but all men followed Him;
Multitudes came to Him to be baptized
With that new baptism, of mystic grace,
First shown to Nicodemus. Were the five
Sleeping in common chamber with their Lord?
Did they, too, hear of sign, thing signified?
To the disciples always speaks He first;
The people, overhearing, get what comes.
How else, seeing He trained these, that, the world,
They should go a-teaching?
                            What spake He here
To the disciples and the multitude who came
(They, too, would tarry on their homeward way
From the Feast), to this green place by Jordan?
"Line upon line," His way: the very words—
Of the new birth, the baptism with water
And the Spirit, the lifting-up should save—
He spake to Nicodemus, these same words,
Again, we may believe, He spake to the crowd,
And chiefly to the five; for such His wont:
Few words and pregnant, utter'd o'er and o'er,—
Lo, here, that Model the Great Teacher set!

To Ænon, where was much water, still there came
The multitudes, to John to be baptized;—
As those three thousand hearers at Pentecost,
Or those ten thousand souls at Travancore
Baptized of Francis Xavier. A Jew was there,
Had been with Christ, mayhap, and heard Him teach

Of that mysterious baptism of the Spirit
And water should give a man life. "Lo, here,"
Thought he, this curious Jew, "two sects!" And he
Disputed with John's following, while he baptized.
Sore for their master's honour, they came to him
With their tale: "Rabbi, He that was with thee
Beyond Jordan, (disciple thought we Him),
To whom thou hast borne witness, (sure, the less
Of the greater receiveth witness), whom thou baptizedst,
(Is not the less baptized of the greater)?
This man (say, Rabbi, hath He done thee wrong)?
Baptizeth, and all men come out to Him!
Like fuming schoolboys, crying, "It's a shame!"
His disciples cried on John to answer them.

From that reserve of wisdom in his soul,
Upgathered in those years of hermit life,
Dropping in speech, epigrammatic, terse,
Whereby a word of John's stands out distinct
From speech of other men, and bears his stamp,
To be known in crowd of all men's utterances
As his, were we not told,—John spake and said:—

"A man can receive but that which hath been given."

Lo, here was peace for these uneasy souls.
All men seek this new teaching? 'Tis of God:
And we—when power departs and friends desert,
How easy acquiescence once we see
Our God is dealing with us! One more fit
Summons He for our work, or bids us go
Up higher in His service—all is one.

"Yourselves have heard me say, I am not Christ;
To prepare, before Messias, am I sent."
(Had they, too, taken him for the Coming One?)

"He is the bridegroom for whom is the bride;
The bridegroom's friend stands by, and hears his voice,
And great his exultation, that he hears:
In this is all my joy fulfilled—I hear.
He must increase, but I must still decrease;
I hear the Bridegroom's voice; it is enough."

What vision was John graced with! He it was
Discerned the Lamb of God, that taketh away
The sins of all the world, in that poor Man
Who came to him for baptism! Now, he sees
The Church (all faithful souls) emerge as Bride
From that rough sea of the world, to the cherishing
Of Him who is the Bridegroom! Hears the voice
Of the Bridegroom in the multitude who came
To Him to be baptized, (in lower Pool).
In a large room the feet of John were set;
In vision was his peace! What else but joy
Fulfilled, exultant, could the prophet know,
When rumour reached him, of his word established,
Of His Friend, the Bridegroom, drawing to Him His Bride!
Then is John further graced to speak that law
Of the Christian's life, his utmost compensation
In every deprivation, loss, and shame;
Sans youth, sans health, sans beauty, power and praise,
Still is this law fulfilled—"He must increase,
And I must evermore grow less and less
Till He be all my hope and all my joy!"—

XIII

John, the Scribe, Saith

THEN John, that other John, the scribe who wrote:—
Needs must it be that Christ in all be first!
He cometh from above, and is above;
No other hath ascended into heaven,
And brought us knowledge of the things of God,
Things He hath seen and heard; yet none believes!
When any doth believe, opening his soul,
Such man sets seal to this, that God is true;
For all that God hath through the ages promised
Perceives this man, with sudden joy, in Him
Who is sent of God, speaketh the words of God,
And on whom is the pouring out of the Spirit,
Without stint or measure, Esaias told of:
These be the signs by which we know Him, Christ!
Such and so great the Father's love for the Son
That all things, life and death, and health and sickness,
Waters and winds, and all the souls of men,
And all ill demons that oppress men's souls,
And every other thing man's mind conceives,—
All these the Father into His hand hath given;—
And more, eternal life for who believes.
But if a man believe not, nor obey,
Seeing the brightness of the Father's glory,
How shall such a wretch escape the Father's wrath?

When Jesus knew the Pharisees had heard
That multitudes, greater than those had sought
The baptism of John, now flocked to Him
To hear and be baptized, (though He Himself
Baptized not, but His disciples), He left Judæa
(Tender o'er the grieved hearts that followed John)?
And, journeying slow, as poor men must, on foot,

He trod sequestered paths and beaten way
(Ah, could we find that pilgrim path for our feet!)
Northward, towards Galilee, where He was reared:
Wherefore He must needs go through Samaria pass,
Hostile Samaria, south of Galilee.

XIV

THE WOMAN OF SAMARIA

THE Son of Man sat, languid, in the shade
The plenteous leafage o'er the cool well made,
For it was noon, and He had walked all day
In the heat of the sun; 'twas Jacob's well that lay
There in the green to invite His noontide rest,
And, as He was, He sat, by weariness opprest.

The Lord was thirsty, too; and for a while,
The need of water might His thoughts beguile
E'en from that spot of ground that Jacob bought
And gave to Joseph; dear to Jewish thought,
And dear to Him Who Israel had led
Through all their devious ways, and in green pastures fed.

He suffered thirst; His living creature there
Lay deep below, nor of its Lord aware,
Leapt high to the well's mouth His thirst to slake!
Never for use of His, the Christ might make
Other than as their wont His creatures act,
Though He an-hungered went, athirst, of ills compact.

A woman saw He, coming from afar,
Bearing, graceful on her head her water-jar:—
Daughter of Sychar she, too bold of mien,
And eyed the stranger o'er with curious spleen:
For every Jew was hated of her race,
And Him a Jew she knew, both by His garb and face.

But His first word allayed her truculent mood:
"Give Me to drink," as suppliant He sued;
And as she drew the gurgling water up,
Gave Him to drink of that refreshing cup,

At leisure she to ponder, Whose that face?
Who is't that asks to drink with so benign a grace?

The woman of Samaria said to Him,—
 "How is't that Thou, a Jew, shouldst touch the brim
Of my pitcher? Through ages past the Jews
All common dealings with our race refuse!"
The Lord beheld her; saw, through flippant speech,
A thirsting soul that craved a draught beyond its reach.

Now Jesus passed her idle chatter by,
And answer made to that sincerer cry
He only heard, uplifting from her heart:
 "Didst thou but know the gift of God, thy part—
And hadst but known Who water begged of thee—
Had been to ask, and get, a living draught from Me."

Dim recollections crossed her untaught mind;
Here was a prophet, sure: one of the kind
Who struck the rock and water issued thence.
What if He struck out stream, to wander hence
To her very door, what labour saved, in sooth!
"Now will I question Him, and learn the very truth!"

"Sir, whence canst Thou get water for my drought?
The well is deep, Thou hast no vessel brought;
Where else canst living water get for me?
Greater than Jacob wouldst Thou claim to be
Which gave us the well, and thereof drank he too,
Our father, his sons, his flock:—and canst Thou greater do?"

How should this soul be taught to comprehend
Water, whose satisfaction hath no end?
 "Who drinketh of this water thirsts again;
Who drinks water I give, shall know no pain
Of thirst, for evermore; in him a well

Brimming with water of life shall spring perpetual."

"A prophet, sure!" But not a thought can find,
Beyond the needs of the day, her darkened mind:
Still harping on that stream of Moses, she,—
"Sir, give me this water, that no more I be
Thirsty, or weary, journeying to the well!"
Now, with long-suffering sweet, He seeks another spell:

"Go, call thy husband to thee, and come here."
The rock is struck at last; a trickle, clear,
Of truth, flows out this most world-hardened soul;
"I have no husband," saith she; and the whole
Of her besmirchèd life is in her view.
Then said the Holy Watcher, "In this thou speakest true."

'Tis no slight thing to speak a shameful truth;
Nor would He try her further, but, in ruth,
Told of five husbands, and another man:
Assured, ashamed, attracted—faith began;
But not all at once would she yield; with woman's skill,
Another theme she opes; "Our fathers, on this hill,

"Contented, worshipped God; and ye would say,
"To worship in Jerusalem, the one way."
And Jesus, tenderer grown for her true word,—
"Nor here, nor in Jerusalem, shall the Lord
Be worshipped, in a near" (how dreadful!) hour;
Confined to no place believe the Father's power.

"Not where they worship, but what men believe
Enables them God's purpose to perceive.
The ignorant, who will not use his mind,
But worships that he knows not, shall he find
God here or there or in another place?
And such are ye; we know; salvation, of our race."

"But comes the hour when not to Jews alone
Condition of true worship shall be known:
The Father for His faithful goes abroad
And seeks them by the searching of His word:
Not clime or nation shall affect His choice;
In spirit and in truth, who worship, shall rejoice:

"For God, a Spirit, intimate with man;
And drawing near in spirit, all men can
Approach the Father." How much understood
This ignorant shrewd woman, of all, would
The Master, lavish of high truth, impart?
To know herself untaught, she had the humble art.

Knew, too, no doom of darkness on her soul,—
"Messias cometh, shall declare the whole:
This thing I know." A mighty word of faith,
Invites Messiah's confidence; He saith,
(Blest woman, graced with News told first to thee!)—
"The Christ, indeed, hath come; lo, I that speak am He!"

XV

THE SAMARITANS BELIEVE

The disciples, come from Sychar, now draw near
With food they had been to purchase for their needs,
But chiefly for the Master's; an-hungered He:
Amazed, they see bold woman of the land
In speech with Him; no Jewish woman, she;
None such would freely talk with man unknown;
Nor would a Jew talk thus with woman strange.
Puzzled, their tongues were held, nor could they say,
"Why speakest Thou with her? What seekest Thou?"
And the woman of their scorn? She was too full
Of the new wine of truth to heed their looks,
Or the pitcher she'd come weary way to fill:
Away to the city went she, empty hand,
Said to the men, (would women turn from her?)
"Come, see a man which told me every thing
That ever I did: can this one be the Christ?"
Full well she knew, for had He not avowed?
Wanted she yet the courage of her faith?
Or dealt she still in wily, flattering ways,
And left the men full credit of discovery?
Whoso's convinced, convinceth: straight, the men
Went out of the city, in the sultry hour
When Orientals sleep, to come to Him.

Meanwhile, the disciples prayed Him, "Rabbi, eat";
Athirst, an-hungered, out-wearied with the way,
Knew they their Master. Who so quick as they
To see His needs of flesh, and minister?
But what is this He saith, "I have meat to eat
Ye know not of." Jealous, they ask each other,
"Hath any man, then, brought Him aught to eat?"
(Now would they glance at the woman, unworthy, she!)

Coming and going, eating and taking rest,—
In these they knew their Master—who but they?
Jesus saith unto them,—"My meat, to do
The will of Him that sent Me; to accomplish
His work appointed." What strange thing is this?
He speaketh with idle woman of the country,
And, lo, that look, they know, of God within
O'erflowing limits of His mortal frame!
This woman of Samaria, what had she
To do with will of God—Messiah's work?
And what hath will of God to do with meat?
They thought it not, but had they let themselves
Give shape to thought, "He is beside Himself,"—
Was ready for their thinking!
                                        Christ, fulfilled
With Joy of him who bringeth offering
To the temple, joy of first-fruits of harvest,
Saith, "ay not, four months yet, and then the harvest:"
(Say not, the season of Messiah's sojourn,
And then the gathering-in). "Lift up your eyes:
Already white for harvest are the fields;
Look ye upon them, see how they be ready!
(All this, for He had gathered one poor soul,
Gain we scorn, in our lordlier wise!
Our Master, teach us Thy humility,
And how a single soul is all to Thee!)
"You have I called to reap the ripened fields;
Good wages get my labourers day by day,
The while they gather fruit to life eternal!
(This woman have I gathered in the hour).
But go I sowing; ye shall the harvest reap,
That I that sow, and ye that reap, together
May rejoice. That saying of weak hearts is true;
One soweth, another reapeth fruit: what then?
The joy of harvest is for both alike;
For both, the fruit they garner: you I send

To reap the fields whereon ye've laboured not,
(My prophets, holy men of old, have laboured).
Therefore the fields are whitened for your reaping."
And, as the disciples heard, they were aware
 As of a cracking of the husk of the world:
Things grew uncertain, mighty, full of import.

And as He spake, behold, upon the way,
A crowd come with the woman out of Sychar:
They came believing, for the woman's word—
(Would we but know what name to call her by!),
"He told me all things that ever I did."
And on that word she came, a reaper, forth,
Bearing her sheaf in her hand—Samaritans,
Who were her neighbours. Boon they came to beg,
That He, a Jew, would come within their city,
Abide with them, and teach as He taught
The woman by the well. Never did Christ
Deny His presence to who craved for it;
He went with them, and two whole days He taught.
And not a word have we of all that store
Of wisdom given to those Samaritans!

But they were worthy, said they to the woman:—
"Now we believe, for we have heard ourselves,
And know this,—the Saviour of the world."
That these, scorned of the Jews, should have bestowed
That dearest title of the Son of Man—
Salvator Mundi—SAVIOUR OF THE WORLD!

INDEX

Of Subjects and references
to Passages in the Holy Scriptures
on which each of the Poems is founded

BOOK I

THE HOLY INFANCY

BOOK II

THE NOVITIATE

BOOK III

FIRST WORDS AND FIRST WORKS

CPSIA information can be obtained
at www.ICGtesting.com
Printed in the USA
LVOW10s1157260317
528501LV00008B/787/P